PUB WALKS

— IN —

The Yorkshire Dales

Other areas covered in the Pub Walks series include:

Bedfordshire
Berkshire
Bristol and Bath
Buckinghamshire
Cambridgeshire
Cheshire
The Chilterns
Cornwall Coast Path
The Cotswolds
Dartmoor and South Devon
Derbyshire
Dorset Coast Path
Essex
West Essex
Exmoor & North Devon
Gloucestershire
Herefordshire
Hertfordshire
Lancashire
Leicestershire and Rutland
Lincolnshire
Middlesex and West London
North London
Norfolk

Northamptonshire
North Wales
Oxfordshire
Peddars Ways & Norfolk Coast Path
The Ridgeway
Shropshire
Somerset
South Downs
Staffordshire
Suffolk
Surrey
The Surrey Hills
West Sussex
The Thames Valley
The Thames Path
Warwickshire
Wayfarer's Walk
Wiltshire
Worcestershire
Wye Valley
East Yorkshire
North Yorkshire
South Yorkshire
West Yorkshire

*A complete catalogue is available from the publisher at
3 Catherine Road, Newbury, Berkshire.*

PUB WALKS
——IN——
The Yorkshire Dales

Len Markham

COUNTRYSIDE BOOKS

NEWBURY, BERKSHIRE

First published 2003
© Len Markham 2003

COUNTRYSIDE BOOKS
3 Catherine Road
Newbury, Berkshire

To view our complete range of books,
please visit us at
www.countrysidebooks.co.uk

ISBN 1 85306 781 4

Designed by Graham Whiteman
Maps and photographs by the author
Cover illustration by Colin Doggett

Produced through MRM Associates Ltd., Reading
Typeset by Mac Style Ltd, Scarborough, N. Yorkshire
Printed by Woolnough Bookbinding Ltd., Irthlingborough

Contents

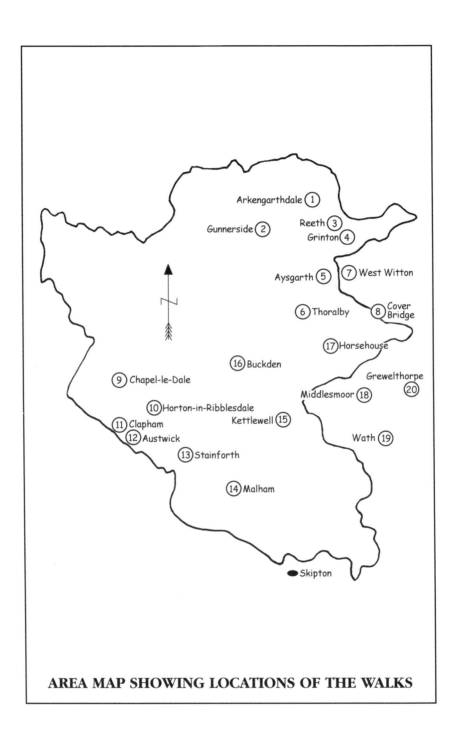

Arkengarthdale ①

Gunnerside ②

Reeth ③
Grinton ④

Aysgarth ⑤ ⑦ West Witton

⑥ Thoralby ⑧ Cover Bridge

⑰ Horsehouse

⑯ Buckden

⑨ Chapel-le-Dale

⑩ Horton-in-Ribblesdale Grewelthorpe ⑳

Middlesmoor ⑱

⑪ Clapham Kettlewell ⑮

⑫ Austwick Wath ⑲

⑬ Stainforth

⑭ Malham

● Skipton

AREA MAP SHOWING LOCATIONS OF THE WALKS

PUBLISHER'S NOTE

We hope that you obtain considerable enjoyment from this book; great care has been taken in its preparation. Although at the time of publication all routes followed public rights of way or permitted paths, diversion orders can be made and permissions withdrawn.

We cannot, of course, be held responsible for such diversion orders and any inaccuracies in the text which might result from walkers trespassing on private property. We are anxious though that all details covering the walks and the pubs are kept up to date and would therefore welcome information from readers which would be relevant to future editions.

The simple sketch maps that accompany the walks in this book are based on notes made by the author whilst checking out the routes on the ground. However, for the benefit of a proper map, we do recommend that you purchase the relevant Ordnance Survey sheet covering your walk. The Ordnance Survey maps are widely available, especially through booksellers and local newsagents.

INTRODUCTION

I've spent many years tramping my native Yorkshire, dozens of pairs of boots having gone the way of the dodo in the process. Worn away and consigned to the funeral pyre – I like to give all my old friends a good send off – that footwear took me thousands of miles across the county, a dozen or so walking books marking out my footsteps for others, hopefully, to follow.

When I first started out as a walker, some of my friends shook their heads in disbelief and muttered 'Why doesn't the silly man take the bus?', referring to me as 'that well-known pedestrian'. But I marched on undaunted, discovering a remarkably diverse, interesting and beautiful Yorkshire along the way. And I kept on walking ... until it became fashionable. Now, I'm having to ditch the lederhosen I bought in Austria in 1966 and get myself a new pair of strides!

Kitted out with new boots and pants, I'm setting off again for my beloved Dales. In four decades I've visited the area on countless occasions both for research and pleasure ... but the enjoyment never fades. In the following pages, I'll lead you on some of my favourite walks taking you to well-known beauty spots and some out-of-the-way places that the popular guidebooks tend to miss.

I love the wild grandeur of the Yorkshire Dales. For me, there's no more energising sight on Earth than the prospect of a footpath snaking upward to join in the communion of fells and sky. Not that this book is a guide to leave you breathless. The twenty walks in the following pages have some giddy gradients in parts but most are from the leisured school of rambling visiting quiet villages, tranquil riverbanks and gently rolling valleys. The walks vary between $2\frac{1}{2}$ and 8 miles in length and no special equipment is needed other than a stout pair of shoes and warm and waterproof clothing for the winter months.

Each walk is accompanied by a sketch map, which is designed to give a simple yet accurate idea of the route to be taken. For those who like a more detailed map, the relevant numbers in the Ordnance Survey Landranger 1:50,000 and the Outdoor Leisure or Explorer 1:25,000 series are also given. Please remember the Country Code and do make sure that all gates are shut and no farm animals are disturbed.

No walk would be complete without a stop for refreshments. Thermos flasks and slab-sided sandwiches are fine in the wilderness but who wants tepid coffee and stale bread when you can have a pint of best and Yorkshire ham and eggs? Enough said. If you really want to follow in my footsteps you will need to haul yourselves onto the bar stools in the King's Head, the Game Cock and the Wensleydale Heifer. It's a rum job! Just one thing to remember though. Even the most accommodating of inn landlords is unlikely to welcome walkers with muddy boots, so leave yours outside.

The majority of walks in this book recommend making use of the inn car park – only if you are a customer there before or after the walk, of course. If you leave your car, particularly outside normal opening hours, please ask the landlord's permission first. A vehicle left for hours in an otherwise empty car park may become an object of suspicion.

Now you'll be eager to be off. So follow my instructions carefully and enjoy your walking. And when you return to the inn have a drink on me. Provided you don't get it ale-ringed, you can use this book as a beer mat.

Len Markham

1 Arkengarthdale
The Charles Bathurst Hotel

This relaxing splash and gurgle dalliance with the sparkling Arkle Beck in one of the most beautiful, far flung and least visited parts of the Yorkshire Dales takes us on a circuitous route to the Lilliputian hamlet of Langthwaite which is widely known through its exposure in the opening credits to the hit TV series 'All Creatures Great and Small'.

Remote Arkengarthdale was once one of the busiest lead mining centres in Europe, hundreds of men bringing a prosperity to the area that has never been rivalled. The miners ripped open the hillsides using impounded water to expose the seams, evidence of these so-called hushes and the attendant spoil heaps and derelict ore processing and smelting buildings bequeathing to the district a modern industrial archaeology. The strange and haunting landscape hereabouts has mellowed with age to become grittily picturesque and compelling. The physician to Oliver Cromwell, Dr John Bathurst, purchased the valley in 1656, his and his descendants' enterprise leading to commercial exploitation of the local ore fields. Some idea of the population count at the industry's peak can be judged by the size of St Mary's church and the Methodist chapel. They can seat hundreds!

Built in the 17th century, the Charles Bathurst Hotel has been extensively restored and enlarged over the years, the recent use of stone flagging and antique timber giving it a bright and modern yet timeless appeal. The hotel caters admirably for walkers, providing excellent accommodation, orienteering skill weekends and a superb base for exploring the miles of local footpaths. In an area where we'd once be lucky to find only ham and eggs, the widely and deservedly applauded CB now provides a cosmopolitan and zestful menu featuring such dishes as salmon in filo pastry with ginger, lime and coriander, mussel chowder, sea bass with spinach, pot roast lamb, steak and mushroom pie, spinach and ricotta pancakes, fillet of pork with orange, lemon sole, roast grouse in bread sauce in season and roast beef and Yorkshire puddings. The house ales are Theakston, John Smith's and Black Sheep. Daily opening times are 11 am (12 noon on Sundays) to 11 pm (10.30 pm on Sundays). Telephone: 01748 884567.

- **HOW TO GET THERE:** Langthwaite is in far-flung north-west Yorkshire. There are two alternative access options. To take the scenic and slower route, go west from Richmond on the A6108 and the B6270 to Reeth, then go north-west on the minor road to Arkengarthdale. To take the faster and less attractive route, go west from the A1 at Scotch Corner, leaving the A66 on a minor road south of Barnard Castle (between Greta Bridge and Bowes) and driving over the spectacular Stang.
- **PARKING:** Park on the verge opposite the CB. Patrons may use the hotel car park – but please ask before leaving your car while you walk.
- **LENGTH OF THE WALK:** $3\frac{1}{2}$ miles. Maps: OS Landranger 92 Barnard Castle and Richmond; Outdoor Leisure 30 Yorkshire Dales Northern and Central areas (hotel GR 999031).

THE WALK

1. Turn right from the inn along the lane for 150 yards and turn right again following a bridleway sign through a wall gap, swinging left and right downhill to a gate.

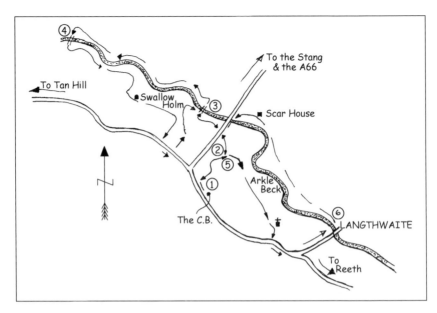

2. Go through and turn immediately left through a second gate on a track, walking on to the lane. Veer right crossing the lane and go through a wall gap into a meadow, following the bank of the Arkle Beck to a footbridge.

3. Cross right over the footbridge and veer left, following the beck bank to a wall gap. Go through the gap and across a meadow, then pass through a series of wicket-gated wall gaps over meadows along the left hand bank of the beck to a second footbridge.

4. Cross left and cross a stile going left, following the right hand bank of the beck. Cross a stile and walk across the boggy land using the boardwalk, crossing a second stile and the line of a broken wall. Follow a fenceline down, continuing on a path above the beck. Drop down left to a wicket gate and go through and cross a footbridge over a gill, veering right towards Swallow Holm. Turn left through the property gates, following the footpath signs (the public footpath goes through the grounds of the property), and keep going forward on the broad track, swinging right by the cottages, going through the wicket gate to the lane. Turn left on the lane for 100 yards and go left, following a footpath sign through a white gate. Pass the front of the cottages and swing left to a wicket gate. Go through and cross a meadow, arcing right to the beck bank. Continue on the outward route back to the second of the outward gates.

The view towards St Mary's church in Arkengarthdale

5. Turn left towards the beck and go first right on the broad path, passing West House and heading towards the church. Pass the church and go left on the lane, walking on and left into the hamlet of Langthwaite. Pass the Red Lion (another good pub).

6. Go left past Stone Lea to a gate. Go through onto a beckside path and follow the distinctive waymarked route over meadows via a succession of gates and stiles to the impressive Scar House, arcing left of the house to an access and a bridge over the beck. Cross the bridge and keep forward, regaining the outward route back to the inn.

PLACES OF INTEREST NEARBY

At nearby **Langthwaite** is the beautifully situated church of St Mary. Built in 1818, its puzzling size is due to the fact that it was intended as a place of worship for the many miners and their families who lived in the area during the 19th century.

West of Langthwaite, at an altitude of 1,732 feet, is the highest pub in the U.K. The **Tan Hill Inn**, where fires burn every day of the year, is well worth a visit. Telephone: 01833 628246.

13

② Gunnerside
The King's Head

Impressively scenic in the first mile, the landscape of this epic walk in the upper stages, to the remains of what were some of the most productive lead mines in Yorkshire, has more than a touch of a geriatric Arnold Schwarzenegger about it. The faded glory and the spent force are still there but the face is grizzled and gaunt, over a century of weathering and vain attempts by Nature at a futile greening doing little to hide the disfigurements of exploitation and age. A sort of industrial Machu Pichu, the haunting scars of the lead mines of Lownathawaite and Blakethwaite are as dramatic a lament for man's search for riches as you'll ever encounter.

Originally a settlement of Norse farmers, little Gunnerside, whose cosy cottages seem to huddle together for warmth, recoils under the folds of its moors. Sitting ruggedly alongside the Gunnerside Beck with views south to the River Swale, it was once a busy lead mining centre, the great ore fields flanking both sides of Gunnerside Gill providing work for hundreds of men during the 19th century. When the digging stopped, many men and their families left for the Durham coalfields, some gaining employment in the Lancashire cotton mills and some leaving for Spain and America. At the hub of numerous pedestrian routes that follow the old prospectors' trails into the vast northern emptiness, Gunnerside is perennially popular with walkers.

A place of warmth and shelter and a source of refreshment and companionship, the English pub, like no other such establishment in the world, takes you home, the friendly King's Head, with its single bar, providing everything but the fireside slippers. As you toast yourself by the inglenook and quaff a pint of best you can even order your weekly groceries, the pub selling all the usual comestibles from a storeroom at the back of the bar. The topography of the Gunnerside area is not for wimps and neither is the girding and generous menu at the Head, such dishes as steak and kidney pie, Cornish pasty, corn beef hash, sausage hot pot and mince and onion pie putting lead in your pencil. The pub serves Tetley, John Smith's, Black Sheep and Daleside ales. Opening times on Monday to Friday are 12 noon to 3 pm (4 pm in summer) and 7 pm (6.30 pm in summer) to 11 pm. Weekend openings are 12 noon to 11 pm (10.30 pm on Sundays). Telephone: 01748 886261.

- **HOW TO GET THERE:** Gunnerside is on the B6270 in Upper Swaledale between Reeth and Muker. Go west from Richmond on the A6108.
- **PARKING:** The pub has no parking spaces available and parking on the narrow lanes of the village is not recommended. Park just diagonally right of the pub door on the spare ground near the bridge flanking the side of the Gunnerside Beck.
- **LENGTH OF THE WALK:** 6½ miles. Maps: OS Landranger 98 Wensleydale and Upper Wharfedale and 92 Barnard Castle and Richmond; Outdoor Leisure 30 Yorkshire Dales Northern and Central areas (inn GR 951982).

THE WALK

1. Fork right from the pub and veer right, following the footpath sign on the bridge wall to Gunnerside Gill, walking along the beckside path up to the gate of Gunners Gill Hall. Don't go through but go right to a gate, walking up the steps for a few strides to a second gate, going through left. Follow the beck up and take a

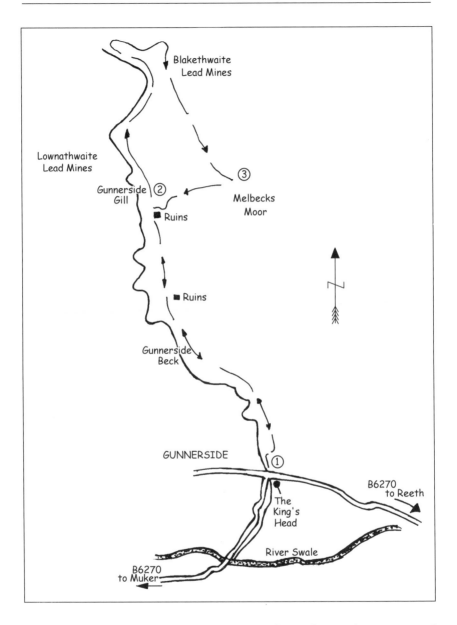

further gate into a narrow wood, yet through another gate and climbing up steps to the 'Gunnerside Gill Woodland' path sign. Keep forward as the scenery becomes progressively wilder and more picturesque and go through a wicket gate, following a path as it veers away right from the beck and returns back to it. Cross a feeder stream on a planked bridge left and pass through a wall gap, turning immediately right. Cross the narrow corner of a field, going through a second wall gap and turning left, following the yellow arrow marker on a stone. Follow the wall left and go through a third wall gap, heading for a spoil heap. Veer left to a wicket gate and go through. Keep forward by the wall, following the yellow arrow marker on the side of the ruin. Swing right and cross a fence via a stile. Weave right to cross a stile and continue to a wall gap opposite a ruin. Go through and swing right. Left across the deep valley, the guts of the Lownathwaite mine spill down the hillside. Pass the ruined buildings (there's a hearth in one) and walk up to the footpath sign.

   2. Continue forward to the beck once more, heading towards a waterfall in the bottom, and follow the beck, passing under the scar and swinging left up Blakethwaite Gill. Swing right just before the dams, crossing the beck on the stones, and swing left and right, crossing Cross Gill, and heading uphill on a track left. Continue to the top of the moor for about $^3/_4$ mile, arcing left.

A stone-breaking machine on Melbecks Moor above Gunnerside Gill

3. Turn hard right on an intersecting track, dropping down the hillside on a snaking path back to the footpath sign. You will pass a number of slag heaps. In the furnace detritus there are traces of lead missed by the miners. Souvenirs! Better than seaside rock. Turn left on the outward route back to the inn.

PLACE OF INTEREST NEARBY
East of Gunnerside is the bustling village of **Reeth**, the largest in Swaledale.

③ Reeth
The King's Arms

This spectacular sortie onto the heights of Fremington Edge follows the valley of the Arkle Beck, giving sky-high views of Reeth, Calver Hill and the River Swale. The path passes through an ancient and attractive deciduous wood notable for rare mosses and lichens before ascending to the edge of the Marrick grouse moor.

Busy and bustling Reeth encircles its massive central green with an independence that has bred its own Parliament. It 'puts the world to rights' every day in the local bus shelter! The largest village in Swaledale, Reeth was once the centre of the local lead mining industry, the production of chert from the Fremington Edge Quarry – the mineral is used in pottery manufacture – also providing local employment. At the spoke of a network of motor and walking routes, the village is a popular base for exploring Yorkshire's most rugged dale, the daily concourse of visitors of all nationalities who stop here for refreshments creating an atmosphere redolent of a rustic Waterloo.

Stone built and as imposing as a Buckingham Palace sentry, the smart and confident looking King's Arms is known locally as the 'Middle House', occupying a prime position overlooking the village green with long distance views down the valley of the Swale. Inviting and capacious inside with ten bedrooms and an inglenook fireplace that's as big as some London flats, it offers visitors excellent traditional and modern fare in bar meal or à la carte options (just down the way is the co-owned Black Bull Restaurant), the medley of dishes typically including lamb cutlets, steak and kidney pie, venison casserole, fresh cod and halibut, beef and Yorkshire puddings and Thai chicken. The house ales include Black Sheep, Timothy Taylor's Landlord, Theakston, John Smith's and Tetley Mild. Opening times are from 11 am to 11 pm daily. Telephone: 01748 884259.

- **HOW TO GET THERE:** Reeth is about 12 miles west of Richmond on the B6270.
- **PARKING:** Park on and around the extensive village green (voluntary contributions for upkeep).
- **LENGTH OF THE WALK:** 4 miles. Maps: OS Landranger 98 Wensleydale and Upper Wharfedale and 92 Barnard Castle and Richmond; Outdoor Leisure 30 Yorkshire Dales Northern and Central areas (inn GR 038993).

The Walk

1. Fork left across the green from the inn, heading for the post office. Continue on the cobbled lane, swinging right downhill past the Swaledale Folk Museum and go left at the corner of Moorlands Cottage, passing several other cottages on a footpath between drystone walls. Drop down to a wicket gate and go through, crossing a meadow between fences towards the Arkle Beck, going through a wicket gate to the water's edge. Turn right on a beckside footpath and go under the arch of the bridge, swinging sharp right and turning sharp right again at the end of the parapet onto the road. Cross over the bridge and swing right past the garage round the bend.

2. Turn left off the road, following a footpath sign through a wall gap and wicket gate. Follow a drystone wall down, walking parallel with the beck, going through a wall gap and wicket gate into a second field to the right of a barn. Continue though a wall gap and wicket gate to a third field, steering right to the top of the wood. Go

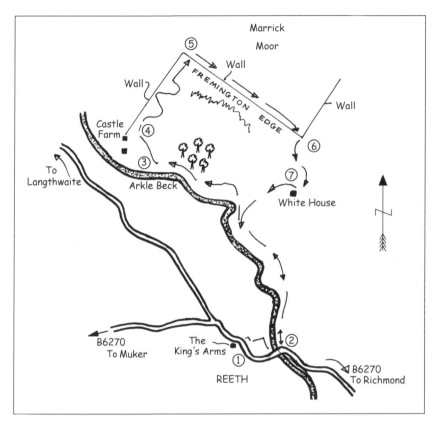

through a gateless gap into a fourth field and follow a fenceline to a gate, going through and continuing on a rough descending track left over a scrubby, woody area to the side of the beck. Continue right, through the wood to the footpath/bridleway sign.

3. Fork right uphill, following the bridleway sign, looking out for a yellow-tipped post and following the successive line of yellow-tipped posts. Go through a gate and keep ascending, weaving left to a point about 400 yards from Castle Farm.

4. Turn right, weaving left on the steep track. Swing right and then left towards the drystone wall, and swing right again towards the old quarry. Go sharp left again away from the quarry, again towards the wall. Swing right and climb parallel with the wall until you come to a wall that creates a 90 degree angle with the ascending wall on the summit – Fremington Edge Top. Cross the wall using the stile.

The ruins of an old smelting mill at Healaugh Side, north-west of Reeth

5. Turn immediately right on a path, following the line of the wall for $^3/_4$ mile to a gate and a track.

6. Turn right, following the footpath sign, going through a gate and dropping down left on a stony path for about 400 yards. Go through a gate to a footpath sign.

7. Turn right, following the sign above the White House (well named), and continue through the bracken, going through a wicket gate and a wall gap into a meadow. Drop down diagonally left, gradually converging with a broken wall and following an arcing track left to the bottom. Go through a wall gap into a field and steer to the right of a barn, following the white arrow marker on the barn, going through two wall gaps and fields to rejoin the beckside path. Retrace your steps back to the inn.

PLACE OF INTEREST NEARBY
The **Swaledale Folk Museum** in Reeth has multiple displays devoted to such topics as stone walls and lime kilns, barns and bridges, religion in the dale, village life and traditions, grannies' treasures and children's games. It is open daily from Good Friday until the end of October. Telephone the curator on 01748 884373.

④ Grinton
The Bridge Inn

This heather-tanged walk over the high grouse moors above the Swale to the top of High Harker Hill gives superb views of the dale, the route briefly escorting both the Grinton Gill and, near the end, the river. The hill was once the redoubt of ancient tribesmen, the OS map marking the sites of hut circles, earthworks and the intriguing enclosed fort known as Maiden Castle. Our path also passes another historic residence. Swale Hall, near Grinton, was formerly the home of the Swale family dating from the Norman Conquest, one of its illustrious sons dying in the Crusades, fighting under the banner of Richard I. This walk is mostly on firm, dry tracks and is especially suitable for winter trekking.

Grinton is presided over by the venerable and extremely interesting St Andrew's church. It is known as the 'Cathedral of the Dales' and once ministered to the largest parish in Swaledale. To the south are Harkerside Moor and Grinton Moor, a wilderness of featureless tussock grass, bogs and abandoned lead mines, the haunting legacy of an industry that once employed hundreds of men remembered only in disused shafts and the abiding litter of spoil heaps, only the wind and the insistent calls of red grouse breaking the silence.

There is something uniquely captivating about an inn by a river bridge, the pausing of travellers down the years to peer for trout and take refreshment inspiring one of the best loved idylls of English life. The stone-built Bridge Inn more than matches the expectations, creating, with the nearby 12th century church of St Andrew, a packhorse bridge over a delightful river and the brawling Grinton Gill that almost washes the old inn's foundations at the rear, a magnet for modern drivers who search out the uniquely rugged and beautiful Upper Swaledale. The inn has an inviting bar and a comfortable dining room serving such dishes as trout with almonds, steak and kidney pie, steak and mushroom crumble, filled giant Yorkshire puddings, lemon chicken and three-cheese pasta bake. The house ales are from the Jennings stable.

Opening hours are 11 am to 11 pm on Monday to Saturday and 12 noon to 10.30 pm on Sundays. Telephone: 01748 884224.

- **HOW TO GET THERE:** Grinton is west of Richmond near Reeth and is best reached via the A6108 and the B6270.
- **PARKING:** Park in the inn car park (patrons only).
- **LENGTH OF THE WALK:** 5½ miles. Maps: OS Landranger 98 Wensleydale and Upper Wharfedale; Outdoor Leisure 30 Yorkshire Dales Northern and Central areas (inn GR 046985).

THE WALK

1. Turn left from the inn and take the lane signposted to Redmire and Leyburn, passing St Andrew's church. Continue uphill for about 400 yards and fork right, through a white gate, following a footpath sign, walking alongside a wall and then a wooden fence parallel with Grinton Gill. Go through a wicket gate and keep straight forward on a track, passing the cottages. Weave right and go through a gate by Beck Cottage. Walk up, going through a second gate, forward on a depressed green path. Swing left to the wall corner to a stile by a gate and cross, taking a rough track, arcing right. The building to the left is Grinton Lodge - now a youth hostel. At the

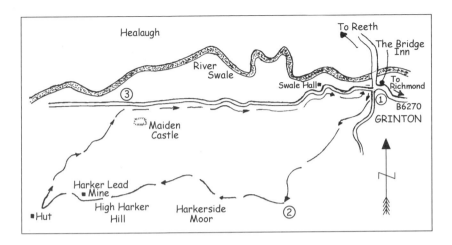

intersection of tracks, keep forward and weave right where the ground levels, going over a stile by a gate. Drop down through the breach in the ancient earthwork and continue downhill to the valley of Grovebeck Gill. Cross via the stones and weave left to a prominent track.

2. Turn right on the track, going through a gate, and recross the gill via the stones, forking right on the track uphill. Veer left and, at

A scene near Grinton

25

the corner, ignore the track to the left and swing right up Low Harker Hill to the summit and a bridleway sign. Swing left at the summit on the broad track, heading for the old spoil heaps in the distance. Drop down the hill right on a rough track and go left towards the hut. Four hundred yards before the hut, swing sharp right downhill and follow the snaking track down through the bracken to the lane and the footpath signs. The village over the river to the left is Healaugh.

3. Turn right on the quiet lane and pass under the shadow of the remains of Maiden Castle hill fort up on the right, continuing for about 1½ miles almost back to Grinton, passing Swale Hall to the left. Approaching the church grounds, go left following a footpath sign down the steps towards the river and swing right, passing by the cottages and the church back to the inn.

PLACE OF INTEREST NEARBY
South of Grinton, at **Castle Bolton**, are the impressive ruins of its medieval fortress. Steeped in history, it is open daily throughout the year. Telephone: 01969 623981.

⑤ Aysgarth
The Palmer Flatts Hotel

Views of Aysgarth Falls have sold more chocolate boxes than Cadbury's, the three spectacular cascades (Upper, Middle and Lower Falls) producing one of the finest natural wonders in the North of England. A Harrod's among picnic spots, the falls draw thousands of visitors each year, film buffs flocking to uncork their champagne at a spot on the Upper Falls where Little John got to grips with the merry man himself in the Kevin Costner film 'Robin Hood – Prince of Thieves'. This stroll visits each of the falls in turn, the route also enabling you to see the less frequented 'waterfall with no name' downstream. On this route, too, is a building of special interest to walkers who have enjoyed Walk 8 in this book (Cover Bridge), that circuit taking in the ruins of Jervaulx Abbey. In St Andrew's church in Aysgarth you will discover a priceless treasure that was retrieved from the abbey at the time of the Dissolution in 1536, a rood screen of circa 1506 bearing references to a former abbot.

Prominently and prettily situated on the A684 with extensive rear grounds spilling down to the River Ure and the Upper Falls, the large and commodious Palmer Flatts Hotel has welcomed visitors for generations, at the end of the 19th century becoming popular for wedding parties from all over the dale. The unusually named hotel has 12 bedrooms and stands, some way out of the village, on the site of a Crusaders' hospice, palmers or pilgrims once taking refreshment and shelter there before continuing their journeys. Today, it is a base for travellers and tourists who are drawn by the reputation of Aysgarth's justifiably famous forces or cascades. It serves varied restaurant and bar meals – typically pork and chive sausage on apple mash, black pudding risotto, roasted monkfish, pan-fried breast of chicken, steak pie and medallions of pork on sage and caramelised onion and Thai green curry. The extensive bar top line up is headed by John Smith's, Black Sheep and Tetley. Opening times Monday to Friday are 11.30 am to 3 pm and 6 pm to 11 pm. Weekend hours are 11.30 am to 11 pm (10.30 pm on Sundays). Telephone: 01969 663228.

- **HOW TO GET THERE:** Aysgarth is between Leyburn and Bainbridge on the A684.
- **PARKING:** Park roadside in the hotel car park (patrons only).
- **LENGTH OF THE WALK:** $2\frac{1}{2}$ miles. Maps: OS Landranger 98 Wensleydale and Upper Wharfedale; Outdoor Leisure 30 Yorkshire Dales Northern and Central areas (inn GR 011883).

THE WALK

1. Turn left from the hotel and go next left down the hill, passing the youth hostel (this old school building became a sanatorium operating from 1907–1947), turning right into the grounds of St Andrew's churchyard. Exit the churchyard, going through a wicket gate and a wall gap, crossing a meadow and heading towards a wood. Cross a stile entering the wood and leave the wood by crossing another stile and continuing on a path, following a broken wall down towards the edge of a meadow above the river. Go down steps to a wicket gate and cross a stile following a footpath sign. Drop down to the riverbank to the first vantage point. Retrace your steps back to the church door.

2. Turn right just beyond the church door and go through a metal gate, dropping down the steps to the old flour mill. This building,

The spectacular Aysgarth Falls

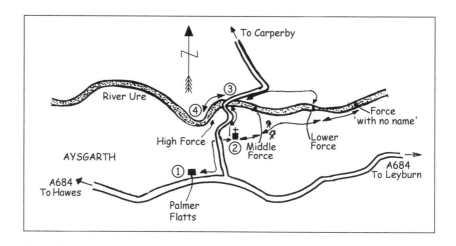

which is now a tearoom, craft shop and a carriage museum, was originally a cotton mill. It ceased grinding flour in 1965. Keep forward over the Yore Bridge and turn right, using the raised footway, following the sign to Middle Fall and Lower Fall. Swing left and cross the road right, crossing over the car park to the left of the Visitor Centre into Freeholders' Wood. Renowned for its hazelnuts, this is the only remaining fragment of the ancient Forest of Wensleydale of any size. Following the distinctive path, visit the Middle Falls to the right and keep on the path, going through a gate to the Lower Falls, visiting and returning to the path. Return to the Yore Bridge.

3. Turn right, following the sign to the Upper Falls and go through a gate (honesty box) to visit the falls on the left.

4. Retrace your steps back across the bridge and turn right at the A684 to return to the inn.

PLACE OF INTEREST NEARBY

The **Yorkshire Carriage Museum** housed in a 200-year-old mill overlooking the magnificent Aysgarth Falls displays a fascinating collective of fifty-seven Victorian coaches. Open all year round. Telephone: 01969 633399.

6 Thoralby
The George

Depending on the season (come in July or August to find the area at its best) this gentle and peaceful old tracks and field paths walk has a colourful start and a majestic finish. First, enjoy a riot of summer flowers along Eastfield Lane – most noticeably the bellflower with meadowsweet, herb robert, meadow cranesbill and vetch in attendance – and, at the end, breathe in the views of lovely Bishopdale ... a memorable outing.

Stumbling across Thoralby is like discovering a Mexican dozing under a sombrero in one of those old-time cowboy films. You want to tip-toe on by to preserve the silence, its lines of ancient stone cottages with date stones going back to the 17th century and beautiful gardens presenting one of the bonniest scenes around. The village is in Bishopdale not far from the popular tourist haunt of Aysgarth, but the masses, thankfully, seldom get this far. Today, Thoralby is very much an agricultural community although in the past, lead and iron ore were mined nearby on High Scar, the village also developing a reputation for hand knitted goods. Even further back, the settlement had a medieval chantry chapel, All Hallows, founded in 1316, the remains of monks still lying in the paddock adjoining the modern house called Chapel Garth.

Thoralby may have always been small and sleepy, but it once supported three pubs! A make-over has made even more of its single remaining bijou inn's simple charms, a recently exposed inglenook fireplace with its log burning stove and spruced up stonework and beams adding to an air of relaxed cosiness that reflects the village scene without. The menu at the George is, however, robust and lively, such dishes as giant Yorkshire puddings and roast beef, beef meatballs with fennel, beef and beer casserole and a range of curries and sauced chicken meals all providing substance. Themed Yorkshire fare, based on historical recipes, is available on selected evenings. The house ales are Webster's, Black Sheep and revolving guests twice per week. Opening times are Monday (closed lunchtime) 6 pm to 11 pm, Tuesday to Sunday 12 noon to 3 pm and 6 pm to 11 pm (10.30 pm on Sunday). Telephone: 01969 663256.

- **HOW TO GET THERE:** Thoralby is best reached from the B6160 – the only road up Bishopdale – coming off the A684 just east of Aysgarth.
- **PARKING:** Park in the small car park in front of the inn (patrons only), or on the nearby lane.
- **LENGTH OF THE WALK:** 4½ miles. Maps: OS Landranger 98 Wensleydale and Upper Wharfedale; Outdoor Leisure 30 Yorkshire Dales Northern and Central areas (inn GR 999868).

THE WALK

1. Turn left from the inn along the lane and walk on for 500 yards to the bend, leaving the lane and keeping straight forward on a hedged track known as Eastfield Lane (also known as Spickels Lane). Continue on this track for just under a mile to the bend near the junction with Eshington Lane and the bridge.

   2. Turn left, following a footpath to Aysgarth through a wall gap and a wicket gate. Cross the first field and go through the gap in the corner to the second field, climbing uphill and going to the left of the barn. Cross into the third field and follow a wall up, going through a gateless gap near the wall corner left. Cross the fourth field, steering up and left for the top of the plantation and

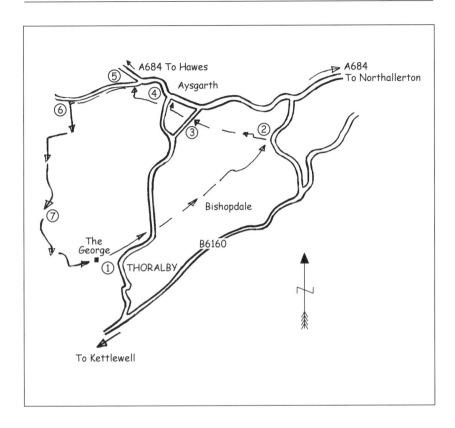

walking parallel with the electricity cables. When nearing the top of the hill, veer left into a fifth field and cross diagonally left to find a wicket gate, a wall gap and a footpath sign. Go through and follow the footpath sign right into the sixth field and drop down to the footpath sign. Go through a wall gap and a wicket gate, following the Aysgarth sign left, and continue through successive wall gaps and wicket gates into the seventh and eighth fields, going through the wicket gate and the wall gap to the lane. Turn left for 20 yards.

3. Turn right, following a footpath sign to Aysgarth, going through a wicket gate and wall gap. Cross the first field to a wicket gate and wall gap and go through into the second field. Veer left and go through a wall gap to the left of the big tree into the third field, heading for the last house on the lane. Go through a wall gap to the lane. Turn right on the lane into Aysgarth village.

4. Turn sharp left by the Aysgarth Garage, using an unsignposted path between two walls and keeping straight forward through wall gaps and over five fields to a track. Turn right on the track to the lane.

5. Turn left on the quiet lane (there is a good view of Bolton Castle north-east from here) and go round the bend for about 700 yards to a barn.

6. Turn left, following the bridleway sign to Thoralby. Walk on and follow the track right 200 yards after the new barn. At the track fork go left, keeping forward and dropping down to cross the planked footbridge over a beck. Go through a wicket gate and steer left to the wall, following the wall up to find a yellow direction marker and a gate. Panoramic views of Bishopdale come into scan from here.

7. Go through the gate and veer diagonally right across a field, looking out for a second yellow direction marker to the left of the lower clump of trees. Cross the next field keeping the same direction, walking on to a bridleway sign. Go through a gate left, following a track, dropping down to a gate. Go through and swing left on the track, descending into Thoralby and back to the inn.

PLACE OF INTEREST NEARBY
The **Yorkshire Carriage Museum** (see Walk 5).

West Witton
The Wensleydale Heifer

This glorious and exhilarating walk with long distance views of Bolton Castle and the valley of the Ure follows age-old tracks and lanes onto the flanks of Penhill, the route visiting the remains of a Knights Templars' Preceptory first uncovered in 1840. Throughout the walk, birdlife is varied and abundant. And our outing also has a musical connection, an ancient trackway taking us to some of the places referred to in West Witton's famous song about Old Bartle.

A linear settlement under the shadow of the mysterious Penhill, West Witton, in the heart of Wensleydale, is an ancient workaday place once the home of farmers and coal and lead miners. In the 17th century, it was famous for the manufacture of butter tubs or firkins. At first glance it appears to be a rather sober and unimaginative little village until you realise that this is the home of 'Old Bartle', a sort of Guy Fawkes/Wurzel Gummidge hybrid who is burnt in effigy every St Bartholomew's Day (24th August). The 'Burning of Bartle' – he is made from straw-stuffed sacking with a painted face – begins with celebrations in the village inns (there are two), the real business of the day beginning after nightfall when the unfortunate dummy is carried through the village in procession. The throng stops at intervals, one of Bartle's attendants intoning ...

> In Penhill Crags he tore his rags;
> At Hunter's Thorn he blew his horn;
> At Capple Bank Stee he brake his knee;
> At Grisgill Beck he brake his neck;
> At Wadham's End he couldn't fend;
> At Grisgill End he made his end.

... before he is burnt.

In its distinctive livery of black and white, the famous Wensleydale Heifer has served Dales travellers since 1631. The inn has expanded in recent years to incorporate what was the village reading room and an adjacent cottage but it retains its ancient charms. Its traditional hospitality is now augmented by en suite accommodation and by a candlelit restaurant and a modern bistro, both providing a range of dining options in addition to bar meals. Speciality soups with homemade bread, gammon and eggs, liver and onions, steak and kidney pie and haddock and mushy peas are all popular with walkers, more formal diners choosing from a menu that includes such dishes as lobster thermidor, roast chicken breast filled with Wensleydale cheese, wrapped in a smoked bacon in a cider apple sauce, lamb casserole with Stilton dumplings and tea scented duck breast with a plum salad. Liquid refreshment comes in the form of Black Sheep and John Smith's bitters. Opening times on Monday to Saturday are 11am to 11 pm. Sunday hours are 12 noon to 10.30 pm. Telephone: 01969 622322.

- **HOW TO GET THERE:** West Witton is on the A684 between Leyburn and Hawes, 4 miles west of Leyburn.
- **PARKING:** Park in the inn car park at the rear (patrons only).
- **LENGTH OF THE WALK:** 6 miles. Maps: Landranger 98 Wensleydale and Upper Wharfedale and 99 Northallerton and Ripon; Outdoor Leisure 30 Yorkshire Dales Northern and Central areas (inn GR 059884).

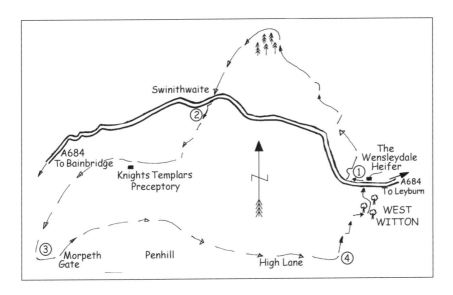

THE WALK

1. Turn right on the footway for 100 yards and turn right again, following a footpath sign to 'Oaktree House'. Weave left and right and go left through a gate into a field, dropping down the hill to the lower corner. Go through the wall gap and cross the field, heading to the right of the gate, and go through the wicket gate to a track. Turn right and go through a gate, following a walled track, going left. In the distance is the looming presence of Bolton Castle. The stronghold dates from the 14th century, Nikolaus Pevsner describing it as 'a climax of English military architecture'. The castle's most famous resident was Mary Queen of Scots who unsuccessfully tried to evade captivity in 1568 only to be apprehended on Leyburn Shaw. It can be seen on the horizon to the north-east.

Go through a gate, following a bridleway sign straight forward and walking beside a wall down to a gate. Go through, following the footpath marker, and head to the right of New Wood, following the wood boundary on an arc left to a gate. Go through and left, following a bridleway sign, on Back Lane. Continue uphill, weaving right through the farmyard to the A684.

2. Turn right using the footway and cross the road in Swinithwaite after 100 yards, heading uphill on a narrow lane and following a footpath sign to 'Templars Chapel ½ Mile'. Veer right and, at the next signpost, turn right, following the path to the chapel.

37

Walkers heading for the Templars Chapel

Keep forward over three fields and stiles to the chapel. Dating from around 1200, this was discovered under a mound. The ruins, a ground plan of a chapel and other buildings together with a number of stone coffins (one is still on site) were all revealed.

Keep going forward in the same direction, passing through two wall gaps in quick succession, following the sign to 'Morpeth Gate 1 Mile'. Go through a series of gate gaps, keeping the same direction but gradually veering left under the crags and then veering right to a gate. Go through on a track downhill to a footpath sign and go through a gate to a track (Morpeth Gate).

3. Turn left uphill and follow this track for just over 2 miles to a footpath sign on the left. Near to the sign, on the right, is Hunter Thorn and above it Penhill Crags. Looking straight forward eastwards you can see Capple Bank.

4. Turn left downhill and go forward through two gates and fields to a track. Ignore the left turn to the barn and caravan park and keep going straight forward towards the wood at the edge of a field. Enter the narrow wood right and veer left to leave the wood, heading left over a field towards West Witton. Follow the footpath past the village pond back to the inn.

PLACE OF INTEREST NEARBY

At nearby Middleham, to the east of West Witton, is the splendid fortress which was the boyhood home of Richard III. In the care of English Heritage, it has particularly good views over the surrounding countryside from its 12th-century keep. **Middleham Castle** is open throughout the year - daily in summer and from Wednesday to Sunday in winter. Telephone: 01969 623899.

8 Cover Bridge
The Cover Bridge Inn

This easy and relaxing walk threads its way through an exceptionally lovely part of Wensleydale and along the delightful banks of the River Ure, visiting the village of Thornton Steward and the timeless precincts of Jervaulx Abbey. A great feature of this walk is the profusion of wild flowers in spring and summer, particularly on the final mile. The path never strays far from a river guarded by a mythical beast called the 'Kelpie' or 'Waterhorse'. Make sure you return to the inn before dark!

In addition to its resident monster, Wensleydale has all the attributes of Middle Earth – castles in wonderful scenery, old abbeys, shivering moors, dark woods and legends of a young hero, for this was the childhood playground of the young Richard III who lived at the nearby Middleham Castle. Yorkshire landscape comes no finer than this, two trout and grayling filled rivers – the Ure and the Cover – forming the centrepiece of a picture that could hardly be bettered on any canvas.

On an old drovers' route, Cover Bridge consists of no more than its river crossing at the site of a ford, and an ancient inn, a hostelry well known to generations of fishermen. Within a rod's cast of the river, the inn was kept for centuries by a family called Towler, who, at the Dissolution, were bequeathed the recipe for Wensleydale cheese by the monks of nearby Jervaulx. This famous Yorkshire delicacy is still made locally. The Cover Bridge and its eponymous inn are an irresistible combination, causing more motorists to quit their cars than an oil embargo. Park up and peer for trout and if you can, for now, resist the temptation to explore the river, retire to the bar to buy your day ticket and discuss the choice of flies with the barman.

A 17th century date stone attests to the longevity of the inn whose beer garden runs down to the stream. Stone-built with low beams and two cosy rooms with open fires in winter, the romantic Cover Bridge has bed and breakfast accommodation, serving wholesome bar meals such as homemade soups, chicken, ham and mushroom pie, steak pie, lamb chops, roast beef and Yorkshire puddings and daily specials like pork loin in a cream of Stilton sauce. The bar top offerings are John Smith's, Theakston, Black Sheep, Timothy Taylor and Two Rivers from the local Hambleton Brewery. Opening times on Monday to Saturday are 11 am to 11 pm. Sunday hours are 12 noon to 10.30 pm. Telephone: 01969 623250 or 622115.

- **HOW TO GET THERE:** Cover Bridge is just north of East Witton, between Masham and Leyburn on the A6108.
- **PARKING:** Park opposite the pub in the designated car park.
- **LENGTH OF THE WALK:** 7 miles. Maps: OS Landranger 99 Northallerton and Ripon; Outdoor Leisure 30 Yorkshire Dales – Northern and Central areas (inn GR 144871).

THE WALK

1. Leaving the inn, veer left from the front door, cross the A6108 with care (blind bend) and follow the road forward signposted to Spennithorne. Cross the bridge over the Ure and turn right on the lane signposted to Thornton Steward.

2. Continue to the bend and keep forward on a riverside track passing an old mill. Go through a gate into the grounds of Danby Hall. Dating from the 14th century, this elegant mansion incorporates an old pele-tower and is the ancestral home of one of

Jervaulx Abbey

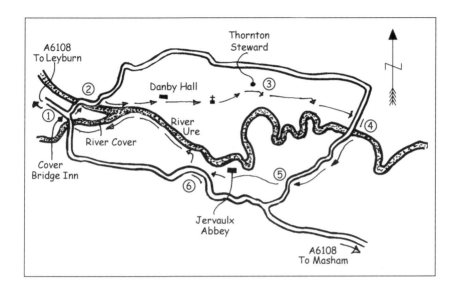

Yorkshire's most distinguished families – the Scropes. Weave left to the hall on the track and go right on a path, swinging right to a gate. Go through left and walk on hedgeside for 250 yards to a gate. Go through and forward into the second field, keeping forward through successive gates and two more fields. Go through a gate and follow a wall down to a gate near St Oswald's church. This wonderful old building has Anglo-Saxon and Norman elements. Continue along a tarmac lane into Thornton Steward. Easily missed in the village is its most interesting building. At the eastern end of the street is a small castellated square tower with side elevations. This was built as an armoury for the locally recruited volunteers who were stationed here from 1804 to 1815 at the time of the Napoleonic Wars.

3. Turn right opposite the telephone box and follow a footpath sign. Follow a walled grassy track to a stile and cross near the vicarage access. Climb the steps, crossing the narrow head of a field, and cross a stile, walking over another narrow field to a wicket gate. Go through, heading towards a wood over a field, cross a stile and follow the hedge down, crossing further fields and stiles towards Woodhouse Farm. Fork right by the barn through a gate and veer left over fields and stiles down hedgeside to a white post. Go left here and cross a stile, continuing to the left of the pumping station and continue to the lane.

4. Turn right over Kilgram Bridge. This was described by the antiquarian Leland as 'the great old bridge'. Walk on right and left on

The delightful Wensleydale countryside

the quiet lane for about 800 yards, passing Park House and going right, leaving the road on the bend.

5. Follow the footpath sign on the track into the Jervaulx Abbey estate. Now in a ruinous state but lovingly preserved, the abbey was founded in 1156 by Cistercian monks in the most sequestered spot imaginable. A model of the abbey in all its glory can be found in the nearby tearooms. Continue on the path past the fishing lakes and the abbey to the A6108 (the tearooms are 100 yards left).

6. Turn right along the A6108 using the broad verge and turn right again after 400 yards, following a footpath sign to a gate. Go through and turn left along the riverbank on a track. Pass the confluence of the Ure and the Cover and continue to the Cover Bridge. Turn right over the bridge back to the inn.

PLACE OF INTEREST NEARBY
Just up the road from the Cover Bridge Inn is the **Brymor Ice Cream Parlour**. Here, you can sample thirty different flavours of ice cream. This award winning delicacy is made from the milk of the cows you can see grazing in the surrounding fields. Open all year. Telephone: 01677 460377.

Chapel-le-Dale
The Old Hill Inn

It's tempting here to look skyward and shirk the challenge that is the mighty Ingleborough. Firstly though, I will take you on a pretty ramble along the dale; but where's the challenge in that? Persevere with me and lift up thine eyes to Yorkshire's only true mountain, taking in the majestic views. Then pull your laces tight, take a deep breath and follow me to a sacred place that was the last redoubt of the Brigantes. Verdant, luscious, all-draping moss – shrouding the amusingly-named drystone walls in green blankets – is a feature of this walk, our route also discovering a wealth of wild flowers and a genie – the intriguing Phoenix of Hurtle Pot.

Viewed from the heavens, Chapel-le-Dale is a filbert in a nutcracker of converging scars, the ever magnificent Ingleborough and Whernside rising to the cracked heights a thousand feet above. Largely anonymous throughout its recorded history, this little settlement came to prominence during the railway boom of the

1870s, the multiple deaths of workers and their families in the nearby construction camps alongside the Settle and Carlisle Railway line overwhelming the ministry of the sequestered little church of St Leonard. The church has two memorials to the dead, one erected as part of the millennium celebrations.

If ever there was a definitive walkers' pub, this is it. It's seen more boots than Aldershot parade ground over the decades. Dating back to 1615, it originally served as a drovers' refuge before welcoming visitors who come to explore the Three Peaks area above and below ground. This newly refurbished stoutly built fortress against the weather is cosy and surprisingly fashionable inside with sandblasted stone walls, exposed beams, recently rebuffed wooden floors and roaring log fires in winter. The inn has two no-smoking eating options – a dining room and a small restaurant – as well as a comfortable and hugely inviting public bar. The varied and constantly changing menu includes dishes such as sausage and mash, beef and orange casserole, ratatouille, lamb shank, grilled delice of salmon and hot boiled ham. The medley of real ales features specialities from the Dent brewery and Black Sheep's Riggwelter. Opening times during the week (closed all day Monday and Tuesday lunchtimes) are 12 noon to 3 pm and 6.30 pm to 11 pm. Weekend hours are 12 noon to 11 pm (10.30 pm Sundays). Times, however, are subject to review according to the season, demand and weather conditions and prior telephoning is recommended. Telephone: 015242 41256.

- **HOW TO GET THERE:** The inn is roadside on the B6255 between Ingleton and Hawes.
- **PARKING:** Park in the inn car park (patrons only).
- **LENGTH OF THE WALK:** 3 miles (omitting point 4, the ascent to the summit of Ingleborough) or 7 miles. Maps: OS Landranger 98 Wensleydale and Upper Wharfedale; Outdoor Leisure 2 Yorkshire Dales Southern and Western areas (inn GR 743776).

THE WALK

1. Turn left from the inn along the B6255 (no footway) for 150 yards and go right along Philpin Lane for about a mile, crossing successive cattle grids, with views of Ribblehead Viaduct on the right. At the Broadrake sign, swing left on a track, going over a further cattle grid to the left of the barn.

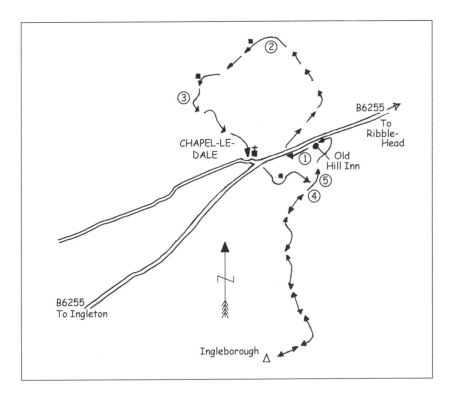

2. Turn left, following the brideway sign to Scar End (moss here), continuing for about ³/₄ mile to Ellerbeck farmhouse. Go through the gate and left in front of the farmhouse and swing right to the cattle grid and the bridleway sign.

3. Go left at the ford on the track and cross the cattle grid, passing Gill Head. Continue forward to find, on the right, the Phoenix of Hurtle Pot – a fascinating sculpture. An inscription tells its story: 'For years, a statue stood on this spot. It was vandalised on Saturday August 27th 1983 and subsequently found in thirty feet of water at the bottom of Hurtle Pot. An enthusiastic team of divers made the recovery and the statue has been erected again as found. It was the creation of the late Charles I'Anson that well-known sculptor and artist. Time will tell if the spirit of the boggard of Hurtle Pot is now enshrined in the statue.'

Walk on (more mossy walls) and merge with a wider track, dropping down into Chapel-le-Dale by way of St Leonard's church. The woodland adjacent to the church is designated as a Site of

The Phoenix of Hurtle Pot

Special Scientific Interest. Swing right up to the B6255. Cross the road and go over the ladder stile, following the footpath sign to Ingleborough. Cross the first meadow to a ladder stile and into a second meadow, weaving right by a hillock under the farmhouse of Souther Scales. Cross a stile into the third meadow and arc left in front of the farmhouse. Go through a gateless gap to a fourth small meadow and weave left to a second gateless gap and a fifth small meadow. Go through a gate entering the nature reserve (limestone pavements), weaving left and following a wall up to a ladder stile. Cross, follow a wall and swing right, following a wall between the outcroppings, climbing up to the footpath signs.

4. Turn right (left if you must!) following the sign to Ingleborough uphill. The route from here is steep but extremely well trodden and highly visible and needs no description. At an altitude of 2,373 feet, Ingleborough summit is about 15 acres in extent. The citadel was originally protected by a millstone grit wall enclosing an Iron Age fort that served as a stronghold of the Brigantes under Venutius who revolted against Roman occupation in the first century AD. Return by the outward route to the footpath signs.

5. Cross a ladder stile and veer left for a gate across a large field and cross a second ladder stile, turning left to a gate gap. Go through onto the B6255 and turn left back to the inn.

PLACE OF INTEREST NEARBY

In the local **church of St Leonard** you can see several memorials to the workers who built the Settle to Carlisle railway – the obituaries to the miners' children are particularly poignant. To the rear of the church, the land is designated a Site of Specific Scientific Interest. It protects a precious fragment of native woodland whose flowers include, amongst others, ramsoms, dog's mercury, wood anemone, primrose and enchanter's nightshade. There is also an abundance of ferns.

⑩ Horton-in-Ribblesdale
The Golden Lion

This classic walk, partly on the Pennine Way, climbs the mane of the crouching lion that is Penyghent. A taxing hill scramble with eye-popping views in every direction from the summit at 2,273 feet, it leads us to Hull Pot, whose cavern roof disappeared in a distant epoch to reveal a shiver-sided black hole of immense size.

Horton-in-Ribblesdale has long been a centre for exploring the Three Peaks country, the triumvirate of Penyghent, Whernside and Ingleborough dominating the local skyline from every direction. For many years, walkers have set out from its post office and general store on a 25 mile gruelling attempt on all three mountains, clocking in and out as a record of their feat. The village is a rugged, wild-west of a place, its massive local quarry and two others at nearby Helwith Bridge adding to the general character of grittiness and independence. Horton has a venerable old church, St Oswald's, with its many primitive Norman features dating from 1120. The parish has the distinction of being the watershed for both the rivers Ribble and Wharfe.

The walls of some pubs are decorated with pictures of local scenery. Such adornment would be redundant in this old inn whose front windows frame views of St Oswald's and the curvaceous lines of Penyghent beyond. With two open-fired bars, one stuffed with gleaming brass tools and examples of the taxidermist's art, the Golden Lion caters specifically for walkers and campers, having both individual rooms and bunk-room accommodation for 15 people. Campers are encouraged to use the rear field free of charge. Typical food choices embrace soups, filled Yorkshire puddings, a range of beef-steaks, lamb rogan josh, chicken tikka masala and battered haddock. The house ales are Timothy Taylor, Boddingtons and Flowers. Opening times from Monday to Saturday are 12 noon to 3 pm and 6 pm to 11 pm. On Saturdays the hours are 11 am to 11 pm, on Sundays 12 noon to 10.30 pm. Telephone: 01729 860206. More sophisticated meals are available at the northern end of the village in the Crown (similar opening times) – telephone: 01729 860209.

- **HOW TO GET THERE:** Horton-in-Ribblesdale is midway between Settle and Ribblehead on the B6479 with main access from the south off the Skipton–M6 road – the A65.
- **PARKING:** Park to the rear of the pub (customers only) or in the 'Pay and Display' facility in the centre of the village.
- **LENGTH OF THE WALK:** 5½ miles. Maps: OS Landranger 98 Wensleydale and Upper Wharfedale; Outdoor Leisure 2 Yorkshire Dales Southern and Western areas (inn GR 807727).

THE WALK

1. Cross the road and turn left from the inn on the footway for 100 yards, then turn right through a gate, following a footpath sign. Go through a second and a third gate to a lane and turn left, swinging right over a footbridge crossing a beck. Go left by the school and follow the lane beckside, swinging right to the barns at Brackenbottom.

2. Go through a gate left and turn left, following a distinctive track signposted to Penyghent, crossing a succession of stiles to the right hand flank of the mountain. Near to the point where you begin climbing in earnest, after climbing the steps leading to the 'FP Brackenbottom' sign, cross a ladder stile and turn left, scrambling over the rough track and boulders to the summit.

Hull Pot

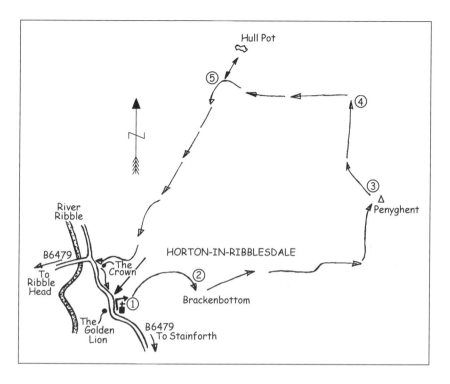

3. Go left over a ladder stile, following the sign 'PW Horton', swinging right under the escarpment and dropping down to the prominent bend in the track.

4. Go left on the track, following the signpost to Horton, and drop down (views of Hull Pot to the right). Cross a ladder stile, going left, and swing right to a second ladder stile, crossing and walking on left to a gate. At this point, you can go right for $1/4$ mile on a path marked 'BW Foxup' to view the impressive Hull Pot. (After heavy rainfall, the Hull Pot Beck charges into the abyss with spectacular force but the precipice is unguarded and is dangerous in foggy weather and should be avoided.)

5. Go left through the gate and continue on a well-defined track through a succession of further gates, eventually swinging right on a track back into Horton. Turn left on the footway to return to the pub.

PLACES OF INTEREST NEARBY
The bustling market town of **Settle** is just a short drive south of Horton-in-Ribblesdale.

⑪ Clapham
The New Inn

Using three ancient lanes, this largely flat ramble takes you plumb centre into Nature's breaker's yard, vast limestone landscapes of scoured, crumpled, crunched and crumbled rock with a few erratics thrown into the mix for good measure, providing a geological feast and breathtaking views.

Clapham is one of those places you can't wait to get away from. It is prettiness itself and bears no resemblance to its London namesake but the lure of the surrounding hills is too great and I'll defy anyone to linger here too long. Clapham is a portal to the delightful limestone wilderness that is the Three Peaks country, the attractions including Ingleborough Show Cave, Trow Gill, the tops of Ingleborough, Penyghent and Whernside, the famously deep pothole of Gaping Gill and the fissured labyrinth known as Moughton.

The large and commodious New Inn - a former coaching house of some repute - sits quietly opposite Clapham Beck, rows of picnic tables overlooking the water providing the pleasantest of spots for summer quaffing. Inside, the inn provides en suite accommodation and bar and restaurant meals in rooms decorated with photographs of potholers and hiking men, the typical menu embracing old favourites like steak pie, lamb cutlets and roasts with Yorkshire pudding, together with more exotic dishes such as Vietnamese style chilli chicken and suckling pig. The bar top line up is Tetley and Dent bitters. Opening hours on Monday to Friday are 11 am to 3 pm and 7 pm to 11 pm. Saturday opening is from 11 am to 11 pm. On Sunday the inn is open from 12 noon to 3 pm and 7 pm to 10.30 pm. Telephone: 015242 51203.

- **HOW TO GET THERE:** Clapham is between Settle and Ingleton, just $1/4$ mile off the Skipton to Kendal road (A65).
- **PARKING:** Park in the inn car park to the rear (patrons only).
- **LENGTH OF THE WALK:** $5^1/_2$ miles. Maps: OS Landranger 98 Wensleydale and Upper Wharfedale; Outdoor Leisure 2 Yorkshire Dales Southern and Western areas (inn GR 745691).

THE WALK

1. Turn right from the inn and pass the National Parks Centre and the entrance to Ingleborough Hall. Turn right by the church and go left, following a public bridleway sign to Austwick. Weave right under the tunnels, climbing up the cobbled lane, and proceed forward on a track to a second bridleway sign.

2. Go left, following the sign to Selside, on Long Lane. Go through a gate (on the left in the valley is the Ingleborough Show Cave – on the right are Thwaite Scars) and climb up (Trow Gill is to the left). Go through a second gate and weave right over the moorland (north-west is the looming presence of Ingleborough), heading for a prominent cairn. Cross a ladder stile by a gate, heading for the same cairn (Penyghent and the amazing Moughton Scars come into view to the north-east). Keep to the right of the cairn, following the broad, grassy track, and keep left, then head right for a smaller cairn where a track from the right meets with the track you're on.

3. Turn sharp right on the green track, heading towards the rocky bluff, and gradually drop down left away from the bluff towards the copse and the farmstead at Crummack. Proceed downhill to a wall.

4. Turn right and follow the wall down to a sign and go through two gates in quick succession, merging with a track – Crummack Lane. Follow this south for $1^1/_3$ miles to the junction with Thwaite Lane. To

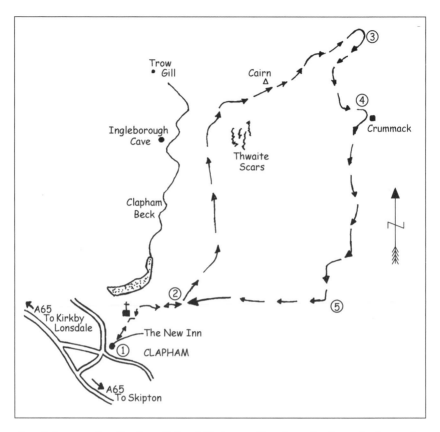

the right, on the flanks of the hill, just a few hundred yards from the junction, are the famous Norber erratics. These are giant boulders. Glacier borne, they were deposited here when the ice melted.

5. Turn right on Thwaite Lane (on the right is the intriguingly named Dear Bought Plantation) for just over a mile and take the outward route back to the inn.

PLACES OF INTEREST NEARBY

Follow the nature trail by the **Fell Beck** to pass the lake where distinguished botanist Reginald Farrer, in attempting to vegetate the steep rock faces of the opposite cliff, filled his shotgun cartridges with powder and seeds! Along the trail is **Ingleborough Cave**, first discovered in 1837. Here are many spectacularly lit grottoes and passages. Open daily March to October and at weekends in winter. Telephone: 01524 251242.

⑫ Austwick
The Game Cock Inn

This refreshing breeze of an amble takes us over one of Austwick's famous clapper bridges to the little hamlet of Wharfe under the brow of towering limestone cliffs. This walk uses a network of old walled lanes – the rural equivalent of a red carpet, which shepherd you gently almost all the way round.

In the midst of glorious limestone country with the famous Three Peaks beckoning on the horizon, pretty Austwick – sometimes known affectionately as 'Cuckoo Town' – is surrounded by inviting hills, notably the well-wooded Oxenbar. An agricultural centre for centuries, it is distinguished by a fine crop of period houses with their Tudor-style chimneys, mullioned windows and date-carved door lintels and a restored village cross at its centre. Austwick has an affinity with the cuckoo, models of the bird taking pride of place in every home at the time of the village's annual street market. Legend has it that the yearly arrival of the bird heralded a period of fine weather. Anxious to capture the sun, the locals decided to incarcerate one daft bird in a stone cage. Before the last course was laid, however, the not so dozy creature flew off!

In a prime position, the attractive and well-known Game Cock Inn has been serving visitors to the Yorkshire Dales for a very long time. Dating back to the early 17th century and with low beams and open fireplaces, it is deservedly popular for meals, serving good, wholesome food in either the bar or its small restaurant, the menu typically offering beef Wellington, giant Yorkshire puddings, beef bourguignon, pork chops, chicken and mushroom lasagne, French Toulouse sausages, steak and kidney pie and speciality Game Cock Pie – a concoction of venison, rabbit and pheasant. Beer choices include the full range of brews from the Thwaites brewery. Opening times from Monday to Saturday are 11.30 am to 3 pm and 6 pm to 11 pm. Sunday hours are 12 noon to 10.30 pm. Telephone: 015242 51226.

- **HOW TO GET THERE:** Austwick is immediately north of the A65 between Settle and Ingleton.
- **PARKING:** Park in the inn car park (patrons only).
- **LENGTH OF THE WALK:** 3 miles. Maps: OS Landranger 98 Wensleydale and Upper Wharfedale; Outdoor Leisure 2 Yorkshire Dales Southern and Western areas (inn GR 766684).

THE WALK

1. Turn left from the inn along the road, passing the school. Walk on 150 yards past the Austwick sign.

2. Turn right by the barn, following the bridleway sign to Feizor. Cross over the Austwick Beck on the clapper bridge and follow the walled track to the junction with Wood Lane.

3. Veer left on the walled Wood Lane (track). At the next fork, keep on the main track left. Walk on, swinging left and right, and pass Wood End, continuing to the road.

4. Turn right for 250 yards, swinging left round the bend, and go left on the private road (footpath and bridleway only) signposted to Crummack Dale. Swing right and left into Wharfe.

5. Go left past the old cottages (notice the date stones from 1715) and drop down on the walled track, swinging right and crossing a bridge near a waterfall on the Austwick Beck. Turn left, going through a gate and passing a barn, and continue to the road.

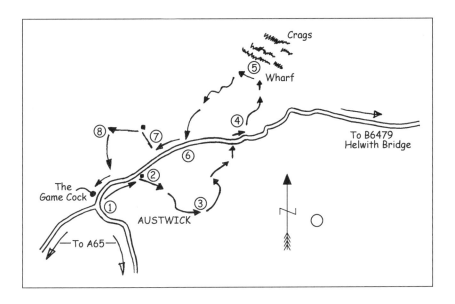

6. Turn right on the road, continuing for about 400 yards to the bend and the stream.

7. Turn right on a track signposted to Clapham and walk up, swinging left at the barn and continuing uphill to the footpath signs (right and left). If you wish to see the Norber erratics – see reference in Walk 11 – stand on the throughs (the protruding long, heavy stones) in the right hand wall and look north-west.

8. Turn left, going through the gated gap through the wall, and walk down the meadow wallside to a wall, crossing by means of the throughs. Swing right and left by the cottage and keep going forward, following the signpost, walking on through a gate, as if through gardens, on a pretty track to a second gate. Go through right and left to the road, turning right back to the inn.

PLACE OF INTEREST NEARBY

Visit the **Dalesbred** furniture and upholstery shop housed in Austwick's old smithy. All the items bear the distinctive ram's head logo. Telephone: 01524 251798.

⑬ Stainforth
The Craven Heifer

There are not many salmon rivers in Yorkshire (even if we have to share this one with the Lancastrians) so this relaxing saunter down the banks of the Ribble is rewarding, particularly at spawning time, the prospect of watching migrating fish tackle a succession of cascades and pools and the famous Stainforth Force adding savour to an already delightful walk. The return route takes us high above the river onto Stainforth Scar and into ancient woodland that nurtures a host of wild flowers.

Quietly situated in the Ribble valley, little Stainforth was destroyed during the Civil War. Rebuilt afterwards using local materials, it remains largely unmolested, pretty cottages, like its age-old pub, clinging to the side of the Stainforth Beck, a sizeable and impetuous fellow that simply leaps from the crags in a spectacular fall – Catrigg Force – just east of the village.

In an attractive and snug position with a terrace overlooking the beck, the Craven Heifer is an inviting inn with bed and breakfast accommodation for the sizeable contingent of walkers who regularly come to explore the surrounding delights of the Three Peaks country. Enhanced by sparkling stained glass windows, its lounge bar and dining room offer generously portioned bar meals for visitors, while its back bar is predominantly the haunt of locals. Something of a trailblazer, this enterprising inn also serves as the village post office. Its menu includes traditional steaks, steak and kidney pie, liver and onions, gammon steak, braised lamb and various roasts. The house ale is Thwaites. Daily opening times (closed Monday lunchtimes, and Monday evenings from September) are 12 noon to 2 pm and 7 pm to 11 pm (10.30 pm on Sundays). Telephone: 01729 822599.

- **HOW TO GET THERE:** The inn is in the village of Stainforth on the B6479 north of Settle.
- **PARKING:** Park in the pub car park opposite the inn.
- **LENGTH OF THE WALK:** $3\frac{1}{2}$ miles. Maps: OS Landranger 98 Wensleydale and Upper Wharfedale; Outdoor Leisure 2 Yorkshire Dales Southern and Western areas (inn GR 822673).

THE WALK

1. Turn left from the pub across the bridge and take the second left, passing the church, to the B6479. Cross and turn right on the footway, going left down a narrow lane after 300 yards. Drop down left and swing right over the bridge (in the care of the National Trust) spanning the River Ribble.

2. Go left through the wall gap, following the footpath sign to Stackhouse. Stainforth Force is immediately on the left. Follow the distinctive path, crossing a succession of stiles, beside the river for $1\frac{1}{4}$ miles to a weir and a footbridge over the river.

3. Turn left over the footbridge and go left again on the lane, rising up to the B6479.

4. Cross the road and turn right, using the pedestrian facility for crossing the railway bridge, and go immediately left along a track signposted 'Pike Lane'. After 150 yards, go right through a gate, climbing up wallside. At the wall corner, ignore the footpath sign to 'Stainforth' on the left and go forward through a gate, veering left on the higher of the tracks, heading towards the distant scar. At the end

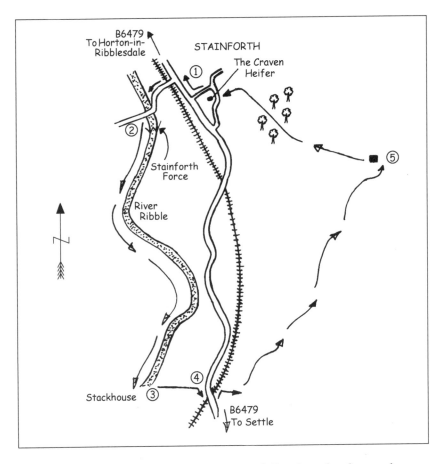

of the walled track, go through a gate, following the footpath over the grassy incline right. Follow the wall up to a gate. Go through and steer right at the big tree, climbing up and veering left, eventually swinging right and merging with a wall, heading towards a gate. Go through left. Keep ascending on the winding path passing a cairn on the right. Proceed just past a gate and go left, using wall throughs (protruding, long and heavy stones), veering right across a meadow, following a footpath sign towards the cottages. Go through the wall gap and the wicket gate.

5. Turn left, following the footpath sign to 'Stainforth'. Go left over the farmyard, following a footpath sign through a gate, and cross a narrow meadow to a ladder stile. Cross and go forward 10 yards, turning right and passing a yellow-topped post (Penyghent

Looking towards Stainforth Scar

comes into view on the right; Whernside and Ingleborough on the left) and cross a wall using a ladder stile. Drop down left following a footpath sign, and continue on the winding path above the scar. Cross the next ladder stile into woodland and drop down left on the path, descending the rough steps to a gate. Go through and keep to the fenceline right, then follow the yellow-topped posts left to a gate. Go through and swing left to the footpath signs, going straight forward through a wicket gate and wall gap, turning left back into Stainforth to return to the pub.

PLACE OF INTEREST NEARBY

The ancient town of **Settle**, where a market is held every Tuesday, is well worth a visit.

14 Malham
The Buck Inn

You'll never have as much fun with your boots on! This adventure walk would get even Indiana Jones's blood racing, the combination of a fairy dell, a spectacular crag that's as intriguing as a watery Petra, and a stupendous amphitheatre of rock bringing thrills aplenty.

With its place in art and literature assured by such giants as Turner, Wordsworth and Charles Kingsley, Malham is one of the 'must see' places in Yorkshire, Malham Tarn and the titanic geology of Gordale Scar and Malham Cove drawing thousands of visitors each year. Despite the attention, this old farming village retains its rugged charms, numerous cottages with typical flagstone roofs, mullioned windows and date stones seamlessly marrying the encircling web of drystone walls, some of which date from the monastic period.

Overlooking a delectable old bridge, the ivy clad, mullion-windowed Buck has been serving visitors to the limestone wilderness that surrounds Malham for over 150 years, its stone-flagged Hikers Bar doing more for the pedestrian classes than the Chiropodists' Guild. The ten-bedroomed inn also has an oak panelled lounge and an elegant dining room, all three dining options serving such dishes as Yorkshire ham, Malham and Masham pie – local beef simmered in Old Peculier ale – fillet of chicken chasseur, prawns and mushrooms in a creamy sauce and roast beef and Yorkshire pudding. The ale accompaniments are Tetley, Theakston and Timothy Taylor. The Hikers Bar is open every day from 12 noon to 11 pm (10.30 pm on Sundays). The lounge bar is open from 12 noon to 2 pm and 7 pm to 11 pm (10.30 pm on Sundays). Telephone: 01729 830317.

- **HOW TO GET THERE:** East of Settle, Malham can be reached from the south by turning off the A65 west of Skipton and driving through Airton and Kirby Malham.
- **PARKING:** Park at the inn (patrons only) or in the 'Pay and Display' Visitor Centre car park.
- **LENGTH OF THE WALK:** 6 miles. Maps: OS Landranger 98 Wensleydale and Upper Wharfedale; Outdoor Leisure 2 Yorkshire Dales Southern and Western areas (inn GR 901628).

THE WALK

1. Go right from the inn for 20 yards then left over a footbridge. Turn right, following a sign to 'Janet's Foss'. Continue through a gate alongside the beck, going left then right through a wicket gate, and keep on the broad and distinctive track. Go through the next wicket gate and follow the 'FP Janet's Foss' sign left for 100 yards wallside to the barn. Go left over the ladder stile and right, following a wall to a wicket gate. Go through, following the yellow arrow marker right to another wicket gate, going through and continuing on a track wallside. Cross a ladder stile and continue beckside to a further ladder stile, crossing into the National Trust reserve of Janet's Foss. (A fairy is supposed to live behind the screen of water.) Continue to the left of the waterfall, and go through a wicket gate to the lane.

2. Turn right on the lane and continue over Gordale Beck, swinging right for about 300 yards to a footpath sign to Gordale Scar. Go left through a gate, following the sign, on a beckside path to Gordale Scar. Wordsworth described it thus: 'Gordale chasm, terrific as the lair, where the young lions crouch.' It reminds me, though, of York Minster at evensong ... particularly after heavy rain when the organ's in ghetto blaster mode. Steer left in front of the waterfall and

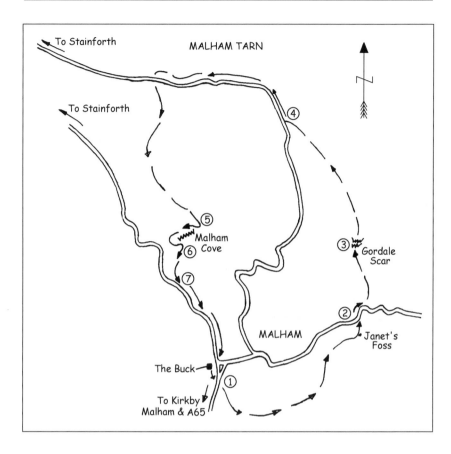

cross the stream, climbing upwards on the well-used route, heading left for the steps. Climb the steps to the top of the gorge.

3. Continue forward along the edge of the ravine, weaving left along the grassy slope. Cross a wall by means of a ladder stile and follow the footpath sign to Malham Tarn between the limestone pavements, steering left towards a wall. Cross through the wall gap.

4. Turn right on the lane and swing left on the bend, following the signs to Settle and Malham Tarn. Walk on to the Malham Raikes sign and take the grassy footpath left (Malham Tarn comes into view to the rear as you climb from here). Cross a ladder stile over a wall, heading for the footpath signs, and stay left by the shallow bogs, forking right at the junction of tracks and swinging right and left heading for the rocky outcrops. Drop down to the National Trust sign, cross a ladder stile and go forward on the stony/grassy path,

The limestone cliff of Malham Cove rises to 285 feet

crossing the broken line of a wall. Drop down and cross a ladder stile, leaving the National Trust land. Cross the next meadow to a sign.

5. Turn right, following the sign to Malham Cove, and drop down, crossing a ladder stile and going left across the top of Malham Cove. This great cliff of limestone, which is reputed to be the source of the River Aire, is 285 feet high. Its top has been deeply fissured by glaciation into characteristic clints – solid blocks – and grikes – the spaces in between. At the end of the pavement, weave left to a ladder stile and cross left down steps, weaving steeply down right and left through two gates to the bottom.

6. Turn right on the broad path, continuing through two gates to the lane.

7. Turn left into the village. At the Beck Hall sign, leave the lane, going through a gate onto a path alongside Malham Beck, and continue beckside almost back to the inn. Fork right across the road to the starting point.

NOTE OF CAUTION

Although no climbing skills are needed to accomplish this walk, the precipitous cliffs are potentially dangerous, especially in bad weather, and the walk is not recommended for young and elderly walkers or those suffering from vertigo. The ascent up Gordale Scar is not normally risky, but after bad weather, Gordale Beck is liable to spate conditions and the climb should be avoided.

PLACE OF INTEREST NEARBY

The **Cove Centre** in Malham is just the place for a spot of shopping. It offers knitwear, country clothing and even a tea room. Open all year. Telephone: 01729 830432.

⑮ Kettlewell
The King's Head

The Yorkshire Dales once had Klondyke fever, the discovery of large quantities of lead ore across the area in the 18th and 19th centuries resulting in a mad dash for profits. Kettlewell prospectors struck their own 'pay dirt' in 1862, a backbreaking but rewarding nine years of mining producing a bonanza of 800 tons of galena from the Providence Lead Mine, just over a mile east of the town. This largely linear walk takes you along the valley of the Dowber Gill Beck with its comely cascades to the site of the mine, the route also visiting a famous pothole - Providence Pot. The miners ravaged the hills with little thought of despoliation and yet Nature has an eternal and subtle habit of reclaiming its own and there is scant evidence of industrialisation save for the gaunt footprint of the ghostly mine, which, in its own way, has the mystery of an abandoned church. Nature really has done a wonderful job of restoration. I wonder what the miners would have thought of the profusion of wild thyme that clothes their old path in July?

With heroic views of the hills from every window, this exceptionally picturesque Wharfedale village, with the sweet sounding name, is as inviting as a singing kettle. Relax and stay for a day or two in one of the many beckside cottages and we'll make a pedestrian of you, a network of soaring green tracks and paths, many of them following old drovers' routes, radiating out to all points of the compass. Kettlewell was once a busy market centre and it is said to have supported some thirteen alehouses to cope with the crowds. Today it is no less busy, hikers, potholers, cyclists and many parties of schoolchildren all converging on a National Park gem that, despite its popularity, is totally captivating and unspoilt.

Prettily situated overlooking the beck and opposite the parish church of St Mary, the King's Head has a large, stone-flagged bar presided over by a collection of stuffed birds and a yawning inglenook fireplace that has long made it a favourite haunt of walkers, especially during the winter months. It serves a varied and constantly changing calorie-packed menu, dishes including halibut steak, beef and ale pie, belly pork, beefsteaks, local sausage on mash with sun-dried tomato and basil, duck breast with orange sauce together with black pudding and Yorkshire puddings. The house ales are Black Sheep and Tetley. Opening times from Monday to Friday are 12 noon to 3 pm and 6 pm to 11 pm. At weekends the inn is open from 11 am (12 noon on Sundays) to 11 pm (10.30 pm on Sundays). Telephone: 01756 760242.

- **HOW TO GET THERE:** Kettlewell is north of Grassington on the B6160.
- **PARKING:** Park on the spare land opposite the pub or in the large car park by the river (fee payable).
- **LENGTH OF THE WALK:** $3\frac{1}{2}$ miles. Maps: OS Landranger 98 Wensleydale and Upper Wharfedale; Outdoor Leisure 30 Yorkshire Dales Northern and Central areas (inn GR 971723).

THE WALK

1. Turn left from the inn, being sure to notice the long forgotten West Riding boundary marker plate that rests inconspicuously against the inn wall. Turn right on the lane, following the sign to Leyburn, and climb up, swinging right to a green near the old Methodist chapel of 1860. Cross the footbridge over the beck.

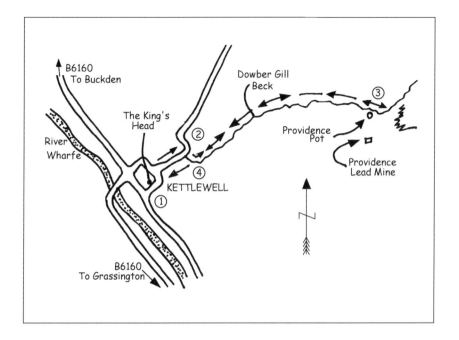

2. Turn left on the track, following the sign to Providence Pot. At the fork, keep right and after 20 yards go left over the Dowber Gill Beck, using the stepping-stones. Go through a wicket gate into a meadow and follow the right hand path to Providence Pot. Cross a ladder stile into a second meadow and follow the wall and beck uphill. Go left over a ladder stile and continue ascending to the head of the valley. Capped with a metal door, Providence Pot is to the right of the path near the valley head. You can peer into the void through a circular hole in the door. To the right on a plateau are the remnants of the Providence Lead Mine.

3. Retrace your steps back to the bridge over the beck in Kettlewell.

4. At the bridge, keep going forward on a lane, following the left bank of the stream down back to the pub. You will pass a succession of cheery and often eccentric cottages that simply drip with flowers during the summer months. About halfway down the lane, if you look over the beck to the right you will see the delightful Chestnut Cottage whose garden tumbles down to the water. Nearby left are the remains of a water mill that once provided electricity for the village.

71

Dowber Gill Beck

PLACES OF INTEREST NEARBY

Just south of Kettlewell, along the B6160, is the famous rocky overhang called **Kilnsey Crag**. A few hundred yards from here is the **Kilnsey Park and Trout Farm** where fly fishing is available, a children's adventure centre and an estate shop specialising in Dales produce. Open every day. Telephone: 01756 752150.

⑯ Buckden
The Buck Inn

There is a cult in Scotland devoted to climbing all of its 3,000 foot plus peaks, this so-called 'Monroe Bagging', named after the lunatic who first attempted to identify every last summit, creating a breed of short-legged Scotsmen whose kilts now show about as much ankle as a nun. In the ascent of this 2,000 foot Yorkshire summit, we will launch our own craze. But beware! This peak has an angular, masculine name that promises ruggedness and virility and you will not be disappointed. Prepare for a hard but exhilarating climb and reserve your assault for fine, clear days when the 360 degrees panoramic views from the top will be stunning. It will take you about 1½ hours of steady climbing; the return, by the same route, will be a little quicker!

During an ill-fated flight during World War Two, an aeroplane crashed on the pike, killing all but one of its Polish crew, the lone survivor crawling through snow and following in the tracks of a fox to safety. After the conflict, the airman erected a monument to his comrades. It has a small effigy of a fox's head at its centre.

Bucken was originally established as a Norman hunting base, the local hills once abounding in deer, wild boar and other game. It became important again during the 18th and 19th centuries for lead mining. At the hub of a network of paths, today it is a great centre for walking and relaxing holidays.

With a front door that looks out onto the hills and the waters of the Wharfe, this old stone-built Georgian coaching inn sits quietly and serenely like a retired general under the martial heights of Buckden Pike, whose invisible top and reputation as a unrivalled viewpoint, draw unwary visitors from the bar. It's easy to become beguiled by its log burning stove and a wide ranging and varied menu which offers such dishes as roast beef and Yorkshire pudding, parfait of chicken livers and foie gras, local sausage on a herb mash, rib eye steak and freshly baked baguettes with a variety of fillings, the bar top choices being Theakston's standard and Black Bull bitters and Marston's Pedigree. So spike the pike first ... then toast your toes and your achievements in champagne! The sophisticated Buck has 14 letting bedrooms and an attractive restaurant serving more formal meals. Daily opening times are from 11 am (12 noon Sundays) to 11 pm (10.30 pm Sundays) although non-residential breakfasts and morning coffee are also available in advance of these times. Telephone: 01756 760227.

- **HOW TO GET THERE:** Buckden is in Upper Wharfedale on the B6160 about 3 miles north-west of Kettlewell.
- **PARKING:** Park in the inn car park (patrons only) or use the 'Pay and Display' car park just a few yards north of the inn off the bend on the right.
- **LENGTH OF THE WALK:** 4½ miles. Maps: OS Landranger 98 Wensleydale and Upper Wharfedale; Outdoor Leisure 30 Yorkshire Dales Northern and Central areas (inn GR 943773).

THE WALK

1. Turn right from the inn and swing right using the verge. Go through the car park and the gate ahead and begin climbing on the stony track. Gradually ascend beyond the treeline and swing right on a track wallside. Go through a gate and keep walking parallel with the wall. To the left in the valley is the village of Hubberholme. The ashes of famous Yorkshireman J.B. Priestley are scattered nearby. Continue to the next gate.

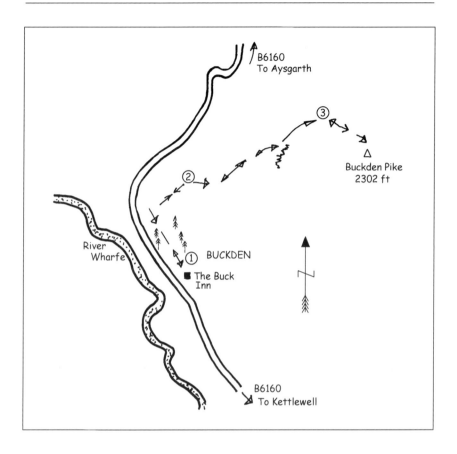

2. Go through right (no direction marker), following the wall right for 200 yards, then veer left and pick up a track, climbing right to a gate and the National Trust sign. Go through, following the path right and heading up across the flank of the hill. At the next two gate openings keep going forward in the same general direction, climbing steadily to another gate, going through and swinging right on a turfy path.

3. Keep forward on a track between two low mounds, heading left over boggy ground for the wall. Continue to the bridleway sign near the wall and turn right uphill, walking alongside the wall, using the newly created series of steps up to the summit and the redundant triangulation pillar (benchmark S5520). At this point you may care to go left over the ladder stile and turn right, following the wall right for about ten minutes to the aircrew's memorial. Return to Buckden by reversing your outward route.

A typical moorland scene

PLACE OF INTEREST NEARBY

In the village of Hubberholme, north-west of Buckden, is the magical Norman **church of St Michael**. There is an inscription inside to J.B. Priestley: 'He loved the Dales and found Hubberholme was one of the smallest and pleasantest places in the world.'

17 Horsehouse
The Thwaite Arms

There are two gob-grappling names to conjure with on this soothing and immensely peaceful walk. Roll your tongue round Gammersgill and Fleensop as you lazily stroll by the River Cover and ascend to the foot of Carlton Moor via Turn Beck. The route follows only gentle banks and gradients but gives stunning views of the heights of Dead Man's Hill and Little and Great Whernside.

Horsehouse, as its no-nonsense nameplate suggests, was a coaching and packhorse train halt on the once busy route between London and Richmond, the hamlet lying in the heart of what must be one of the least visited dales in the county – a dale described by the writer Ella Pontefract as '…one of Wensleydale's alien children'. At just 12 miles long on a minor, twisting, narrow road with no obvious tourist destination to encourage visitors, Coverdale is a shy and retiring valley of wide skies and solitude, only its reclusive river, and the grouse, curlews and golden plover on the wild moors above, breaking the silence. This bonny little place must be one of the few places in England that can boast of less traffic now than two centuries ago.

There were two inns to serve the coaches and the packhorse trains of up to forty sweating beasts that regularly passed through Horsehouse, the dapper Thwaite Arms continuing its role with a little more refinement than in the days of old. It sits prettily opposite the church of St Botolph, its twin, simply-furnished bars offering wholesome bar meals such as steak and kidney pie, beef casserole, vegetable and bean hot pot and Sunday roasts. The house ales are Theakston and John Smith's. The inn is closed Monday lunchtimes. Opening times during the rest of the week (but grandfather clocks in Horsehouse have been known to nod off so it's best to check with the landlord first) are Monday evening 7 pm to 11 pm, Tuesday to Friday 12 noon to 2 pm and 7 pm to 11 pm. Weekend hours are 12 noon to 3 pm and 7 pm to 11 pm (10.30 pm on Sunday). The inn has a camping field nearby. Telephone: 01969 640206.

- **HOW TO GET THERE:** Horsehouse is in Coverdale. The best access is from the east, taking the minor road south-west from the A6108 at Middleham, passing through Carlton.
- **PARKING:** There is no parking to speak of at the inn. Park at the side of the lane.
- **LENGTH OF THE WALK:** 5 miles. Maps: OS Landranger 98 Wensleydale and Upper Wharfedale; Outdoor Leisure 30 Yorkshire Dales Northern and Central areas (inn GR 048813).

THE WALK

1. Turn left from the inn and go immediately left again by its gable wall on a track in front of the cottages for 75 yards, then turn right, following a footpath sign down to a gate and a second sign marked to 'Gammersgill 1 Mile'. Go left through the gate over four meadows and through their gates, following the yellow arrow markers towards the riverbank.

2. Follow the bank downstream, crossing four stiles and one planked bridge over a feeder stream to the 'FP Gammersgill' sign. Ignore this and keep to the river bank, arcing left to go through a wicket gate and two subsequent wicket gates, following the yellow arrow markers. Then steer left across a field away from the river, heading towards Hall Farm and a gate. Cross a stile and a field below

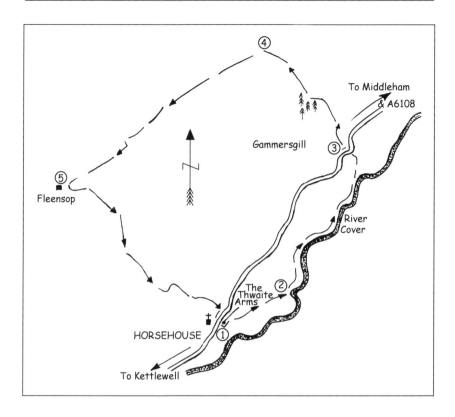

the farmhouse, heading for a yellow-tipped post in a wall. Cross a wall stile and weave between the trees to the lane.

3. Turn right on the lane, swinging right opposite Bridge End Farm, and go left through a gate, following a footpath marked to 'Fleensop via High Field'. Go forward over a field and go through a gate to a footpath sign. Turn right. Follow a wall and swing left to a gate. Go right, following a footpath sign through a gate, and drop down to cross the Turn Beck on stepping stones, climbing up left towards the edge of the conifer plantation, then accompanying a Turn Beck feeder stream right to a wall gap and wicket gate. Go through and immediately left to a stile, then turn right by the side of a ruin, weaving left across a small field to a wall gap. Go through and turn right, following a footpath sign and heading for the intersection of walls, walking left through the tussock grass towards a gate.

4. Turn left over a stile and cross a second stile by a gate, following a yellow arrow marker and a footpath sign, ignoring the

79

Horsehouse School

track to the right. Continue through the tussock grass and go through a wicket gate keeping forward, weaving right to cross the Turn Beck using the stepping stones. Go through a wicket gate left (hidden) and swing right going up the bank, following the valley of the beck up. Weave left through the tussock grass to a footpath sign. Go through a wicket gate and keep forward, heading towards the top of the conifer plantation. Cross the next wall via a ladder stile and drop down the dip, rising again and heading towards a wall. Swing right by the wall to a gate just before the tip of the triangular-shaped plantation. Go left through the gate and steer right across the meadow to a gate. Go through right and follow the footpath sign, heading left to the top corner of a barn. Swing left by the barn to a gate and go through right, keeping forward on a track, going through two more gates in quick succession. Go through another gate heading for Fleensop, dropping down and swinging hard left in an arc to the farm buildings. Less than a mile to the south-west there was once a colliery.

5. Continue on the metalled access road for 150 yards and fork right, going through a gate, following a sign to 'Horsehouse 1¼ Miles'. Head up the hill left, aiming for the top corner of the plantation. At the corner, go left over a stile to a wall and turn right, following the line of the wall uphill. Weave right at the top to a gate and go through left. (Dead Man's Hill, and Little and Great Whernside come into prominence here.) Walk downhill, weaving right over a rough field between the stands of tussock grass, heading for a wall corner, and follow the wall down, keeping forward over boggy ground (the path soon improves). Follow the wall as it arcs left to a ladder stile and cross, swinging right and dropping down at the side of High Gill on a rough track. Follow the track as it widens, down to a stile. Cross and walk onto the lane, turning right back to the inn.

PLACE OF INTEREST NEARBY

In Coverdale, you will find **The Forbidden Corner** – the word fantastic is overworked but not here! In a unique four-acre garden, you will discover labyrinths, dark tunnels, secret chambers, follies, and multiple strange surprises from the nether world. It is open every day from April to October and then Sundays until Christmas. Tickets must be pre-booked by phoning 01969 640638/640687.

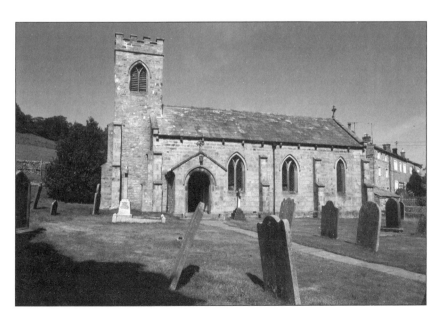

The village church in Horsehouse

81

⑱ Middlesmoor
The Crown Hotel

Along the line of the old drovers' road, our route leads over the moor to the spectacular Scar House and Angram Reservoirs. Below the monumental Scar House is the site of the construction workers' self-contained town, remnants of which can still be seen. Crossing the dam top, the path, newly opened by Yorkshire Water, leads to the foot of Dead Man's Hill – the site of a string of grisly murders – and skirts the shoreline to the twin dam of Angram, crossing its dam top. The area has a wild grandeur, the rarest of our national birds – the golden eagle – sometimes gracing its skies. On the day of my last visit, I saw basking lizards.

Perched at the head of Nidderdale with long distance views down its valley, Middlesmoor is more a rocky redoubt than a village. Up there with the grouse and golden plovers on a 900 foot hilltop, it once earned a precarious living from farming and mining, construction work on the nearby Bradford Corporation dams of Angram and Scar House (completed in 1918 and 1936 respectively) bringing only temporary prosperity. Today, the stone built village with its winding streets and church, which was restored in the 1860s, serves as a Yorkshire version of a Nepalese hill-station, revictualling walkers, some of whom make the exciting trek from Pateley Bridge along the track of the old narrow-gauge dams' railway heading for Dead Man's Hill and Coverdale beyond the skyline.

Originally constructed in the 18th century, the welcoming Crown Hotel has witnessed mixed fortunes in the past few decades. Lacking trade, it was shut for a while, but today, thanks to the influx of walkers, it's back to its busy self, offering overnight accommodation in seven bedrooms and girding refreshments such as beefsteaks, steak and kidney pie, home cooked ham and roast beef and Yorkshire puddings. This jolly little inn is proud of its roots, a collection of nostalgic photographs mostly donated by local residents – one picture shows the men of Angram shearing sheep before their pastures were flooded forever – gracing its twin bars which flicker with open fires during the winter months. It serves Black Sheep, John Smith's and Theakston bitters. Opening times are 12 noon to 3 pm (closed Monday lunchtimes) and 7 pm to 11 pm (10.30 pm on Sundays). Telephone: 01423 755204.

- **HOW TO GET THERE:** Middlesmoor is conspicuously located at the head of Nidderdale. Take the minor road from Pateley Bridge (on the B6265 between Ripon and Skipton) following the right bank of the River Nidd, past Gouthwaite Reservoir and through the villages of Ramsgill and Lofthouse.
- **PARKING:** There is a small parking area for customers in front of the pub. There is also a visitors' car park up the street on the right. At busy periods at the height of summer, however, parking can be a problem in Middlesmoor. Alternatively, there is a fee paying car park over the Nidd river bridge at How Stean Gorge.
- **LENGTH OF THE WALK:** 8 miles. Maps: OS Landrangers 98 Wensleydale and Upper Wharfedale and 99 Northallerton and Ripon; Outdoor Leisure 30 Yorkshire Dales Northern and Central areas (inn GR 092742).

THE WALK

1. Turn left from the inn on the lane and merge with a stony track, continuing straight forward for about $1^3/_4$ miles. Behind is a wonderful vista of Gouthwaite Reservoir in the far distance. Over the

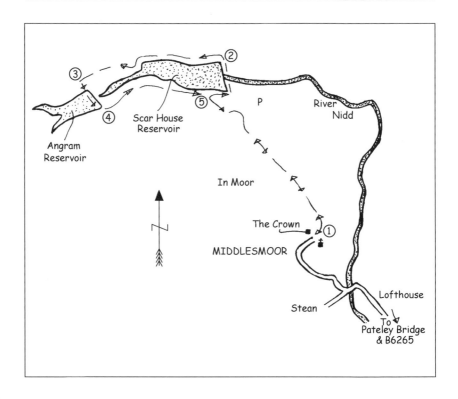

grouse butts, the mass of Great Whernside comes into view on the left. The hill in front is Dead Man's Hill, so called because an evil innkeeper murdered several Scottish guests in their beds, stealing their money and tartans. Go through a gate and walk on down the winding and descending track to the dam wall of Scar House Reservoir and cross, using the dam top footway. Far below to the right, is the site of the construction workers' town. At one time, it had a population of 1,250. The dam is 233 feet high and the reservoir contains some 2,215 million gallons of water.

2. Turn left, following the well-defined, signposted path along the shoreline. Cross a stile near the walkers' shelter towards the far end of the reservoir and steer right on the winding path, heading for the right hand side of Angram's dam top.

3. Turn left over the dam wall.

4. Turn left again on the access track and continue back to Scar House dam.

5. Turn right and retrace your steps uphill back to the inn.

Scar House Dam

PLACE OF INTEREST NEARBY
How Stean Gorge, which can be found by turning first right after descending the hill from Middlesmoor, is an 80 foot ravine with narrow paths, Indiana Jones-type bridges and an easily explored cave. There is also a small restaurant available. Open March to January. Telephone: 01423 755666.

⑲ Wath
The Sportsman's Arms

Not for the bronchially challenged, this interest-packed Ferris wheel of a walk will initially have you gasping skywards to contemplate some of the finest views in the county taking in Gouthwaite Reservoir, Great Whernside and the rocket scanning surveillance technology that is Menwith Hill. The route leads through the long abandoned Scotgate Quarry, its valuable and hard-wearing stone having gone to create half of Pateley Bridge and parts of Hull Docks, St Paul's Cathedral and Number 10 Downing Street. The latter, gentler stretch of the circuit takes us along the former track of the Nidderdale Light Railway – it was built to service the construction of the Angram and Scar House Reservoirs in the upper dale – following the pretty and thoroughly relaxing course of the River Nidd with its kingfishers and dippers.

Tucked beneath a fold of the surrounding hills just a few yards from an impossibly impractical packhorse bridge and a river dimpled by trout, the immensely inviting 17th century Sportsman's Arms is like a favourite grandfather clock. Buffed and burnished with the smell of beeswax, it ticks on in that slow and incomparably English way, marvellously archaic wintertime coal and log fires and candlelight adding to a timeless sense of hospitality that could come straight from a novel by Walpole or Hardy. In a Conservation Village and an area designated as being of outstanding natural beauty, it is located in one of the least commercial parts of the Dales, offering accommodation in 12 en suite bedrooms, a restaurant, morning coffees and bar meals such as tomato and chive soup, oak chicken with mango and salad, calf's liver on mash, beefsteak with a blue Yorkshire cheese sauce, crumbed pork loin and roasted apple with a cream and plum sauce and roast Whitby codling. Served in the back bar which is handsomely decorated with plaster cast fishing trophies and clocks, the house ales are Theakston and John Smith's. Opening hours are 12 noon to 2 pm and 6.30 pm to 11 pm (10.30 pm on Sundays). Telephone: 01423 711306.

- **HOW TO GET THERE:** Wath is around 2 miles north-west of Pateley Bridge. Cross the river and take the signposted road to Lofthouse and Middlesmoor then go right over the packhorse bridge.
- **PARKING:** Park in the inn car park (patrons only).
- **LENGTH OF THE WALK:** 3½ miles. Maps: OS Landranger 99 Northallerton and Ripon; Explorer 298 Nidderdale, Ripon and Pateley Bridge (inn GR 145678).

THE WALK

1. Leave the inn left across the car park and turn left along the lane, walking on uphill right passing the cottages and the Methodist chapel and swinging left uphill.

2. Immediately after Windy Nook cottage turn sharp left on the steeply inclined lane and climb up, swinging right. There are stunning views back from here north-west looking over Gouthwaite Reservoir. Continue going forward at the junction of lanes, ignoring the right hand turn, and keep ascending for about 500 yards. To the right, on the skyline, are the highly secret radar domes (Star Wars technology) of Menwith Hill.

3. Turn off the lane right, just past the small conifer plantation to the left, through a gate, following a public footpath sign and veering left over the top of a field. Go left through a wall gap and a gateless

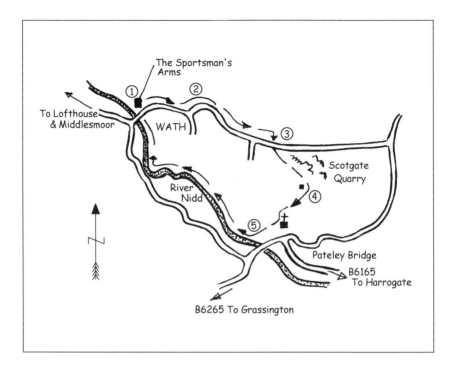

opening, continuing on a rough track through the massive abandoned quarry – Scotgate Quarry. Drop down to the left of the old farmhouse and Scotgate Cottage and continue for about 300 yards.

4. Turn right, following a public footpath sign to Pateley Bridge, going through a gate and dropping down wallside. Cross a stile and keep forward on a rough track, swinging left on a more substantial access way that eventually becomes an ever-widening lane. Turn left on Wath Road towards the church of St Cuthbert and swing right downhill past the police station. To the right opposite the church is the Nidderdale Museum offering insights into local history.

5. Turn right on King Street by the fish and chip shop and go almost immediately left down Millfield Street. Go left again and follow the 'Nidderdale Way' sign. Weave right and walk forward to the end of the cul-de-sac, continuing on the riverside path, passing the weir. Weave through the Pateley Bridge Millennium Green on the footpath and continue on the riverside path, passing a stone revetment to the right – remains of the Nidderdale Light Railway. As

Looking back over Wath to Gouthwaite Reservoir

you approach Wath, head towards the river to the left of the treatment works across the meadow to find a footbridge over a stream near the old packhorse bridge. Cross and go right on the lane back to the inn.

PLACE OF INTEREST NEARBY

In King Street, at Pateley Bridge, you will find the **Nidderdale Museum**. It has multiple exhibits depicting local agricultural and industrial life, housed in twelve rooms of a former Victorian workhouse. It is open daily from Easter to November and then weekends only from November to Easter. Telephone: 01423 711225.

20 Grewelthorpe
The Crown

If rampant nature is your thing, this is the walk for you, a profusion of wonderfully errant trees, shrubs and wild flowers providing a rewarding ramble to one of the most picturesque yet least visited beauty spots in the county. And it has a golden beach! This place has brought out the best in poets and artists, a famous canvas by Turner capturing the drama of a verdant river gorge set out in the 19th century by William Aislabie as a 'wilderness garden' complete with waterfalls, pools and a range of follies. For a time the woodland, known as Hackfall, was threatened by commercial logging but it was thankfully saved for the nation by the Woodland Trust who have now embarked on a long-term programme of maintenance and repair.

Grewelthorpe is only a few miles from the tourist haunt of Masham and yet it remains totally unspoilt. Amazingly though, over a century ago it witnessed visitors by the carriage load, the lure of Hackfall, the grandeur of its scenery and the chance to take tea in the romantic Fisher's Hall, drawing fee-paying customers from all parts of the north. Hackfall was designed as a deliberate contrast to the formality of the planting at nearby Fountains Abbey, its inspiration coming from Aislabie's tour of the Alps. Now totally wild and largely unchecked, the woodland has a leafy canopy that could not be bettered in Amazonia.

On an old packhorse route between Masham and Kirkby Malzeard – note the retained archway that once led to the rear stables – the attractive stone-built Crown is on the main street in the centre of Grewelthorpe. With an attractive L-shaped bar, a rear dining room and a beer garden overlooking its own quoits pitch, the Crown gives a number of dining choices, the ever-changing menu embracing such dishes as homemade soups, game terrine, steak and kidney casserole, Whitby whole tail scampi, chargrilled chicken, port wine steaks, crispy duck strips on black pudding and goat's cheese and traditional Sunday lunches. The bar top line up is Black Sheep and John Smith's. Opening times (closed Monday lunchtimes) are 12 noon to 3 pm and 7 pm to 11 pm (10.30 pm on Sundays). Telephone: 01765 658210.

- **HOW TO GET THERE:** Grewelthorpe is on the minor road between Masham (A6108) and Kirkby Malzeard.
- **PARKING:** Park in the car park to the rear of the pub through the archway (patrons only).
- **LENGTH OF THE WALK:** 3½ or 6 miles. Maps: OS Landranger 99 Northallerton and Ripon; Explorer 298 Nidderdale, Ripon and Pateley Bridge (inn GR 231763).

THE WALK

NB: Some of the paths in the woodland are steep and they can be muddy and slippery in wet weather.

1. Turn right from the inn along the street heading north and pass the church, taking the forked lane left signposted to Ilton. Continue on the lane for 200 yards and turn right, following a footpath sign over a meadow veering right. Cross several stiles, heading in the same direction, to the edge of Oak Bank Wood. Turn right through a gate and walk downhill on the edge of the wood (keep a drystone wall to your right) to join a track. Turn right on the track and continue to the Masham road.

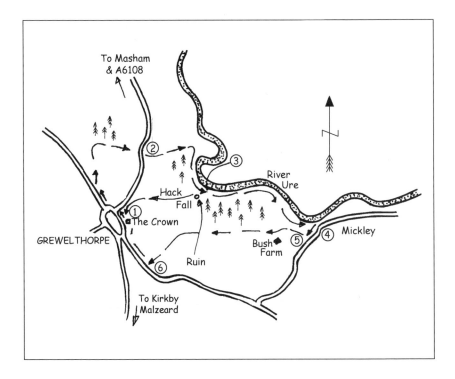

2. Cross the road and take the signposted track to Hackfall, dropping down to the Woodland Trust sign. Notice the spectacular long distance views to the north-east. Enter the wood and drop down, arcing right. Walk on, following the winding riverside path. Pass the beach on your left and continue on the winding track uphill to the octagonal lancet windowed ruin known as Fisher's Hall on a little promontory overlooking the river. Note the use of tufa in its construction and the initials 'WA' on a stone above the entrance. From here, you can choose either to return to Grewelthorpe (the track goes south-west uphill, companioning a stream to Hackfall Farm and the village) or to continue along the riverside path to enjoy more of the wood as follows:

3. Drop down left from the ruin and follow the path over a stream, climbing again right. Continue on the well-defined, winding path for another mile or so to emerge on a lane.

4. Turn right on the lane uphill for about 400 yards.

5. Turn right off the lane, crossing a stile, and follow a footpath sign down the edge of a field. Then bear left, dropping down and

Taking a rest in Hackfall Woods

crossing a dip in the land, rising up right to a gate. Go through and keep to the right of Bush Farm on a path going west through a succession of gated fields to a stile. Cross and follow the hedgeline down to a gate. Go through right and follow a walled track left to the lane.

6. Turn right through Grewelthorpe back to the inn.

PLACES OF INTEREST NEARBY

Two miles away at Masham are the **Masham Craft Workshops**. Hand-made glass, domestic stoneware pottery and unique gold and silver jewellery are all available. The workshops are generally open daily from Easter to October. The **Black Sheep Brewery Visitor Centre**, also in Masham, offers year-round tours and sampling. Telephone: 01765 689057.